THE

NOTRE DAME®

BOOK of PRAYER

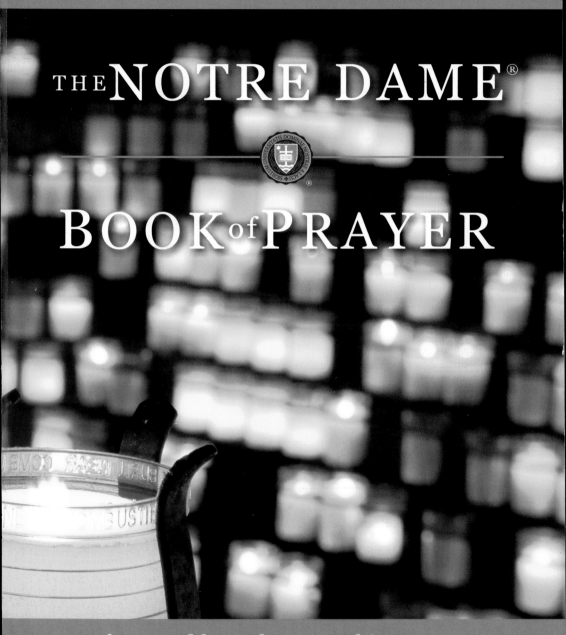

Foreword by Theodore M. Hesburgh, C.S.C.

THE NOTRE DAME®

BOOK of PRAYER

Afterword by John I. Jenkins, C.S.C.

Office of Campus Ministry

Edited by Heidi Schlumpf ✣ Photographs by Matt Cashore

Imprimatur: Most Reverend John M. D'Arcy
    Bishop of Fort Wayne–South Bend
Nihil Obstat: Reverend Monsignor Michael Heintz, PhD
    Censor Librorum
    Given in Fort Wayne, Indiana, on 10 January 2010.

Founded in 1865, Ave Maria Press is a ministry of the Indiana Province of Holy Cross.

www.avemariapress.com

ISBN-10 1-59471-196-8   ISBN-13 978-1-59471-196-1

Interior images © Matt Cashore.

Cover and text design by John R. Carson.

Printed and bound in the United States of America.

Library of Congress Cataloging-in-Publication Data
The Notre Dame book of prayer / Office of Campus Ministry ; edited by Heidi Schlumpf.
    p. cm.
Includes bibliographical references and index.
ISBN-13: 978-1-59471-196-1 (hardcover : alk. paper)
ISBN-10: 1-59471-196-8 (hardcover : alk. paper)
1. Universities and colleges--Prayers. 2. University of Notre Dame--Religion. 3. Prayers--Christianity. I. Schlumpf, Heidi. II. University of Notre Dame. Office of Campus Ministry.
BV283.C7N68 2010
242'.802--dc22
                              2010019402

✧ CONTENTS ✧

✣ FOREWORD ✣

Lord, teach us to pray, just as John taught his disciples.
—Luke 11:1

On the Notre Dame campus and throughout the world, I have found that young people have maintained the same deep yearning for a full and profoundly meaningful connection with God that the apostles displayed in their request to Jesus, "Lord, teach us to pray." They, in deep communion with people of every place and age, express a hunger for prayer that is often coupled with feelings of dissatisfaction with their present prayer life. I can imagine that our young Notre Dame graduates, sent forth from the prayerful structure of campus, must often wonder how to be holy people confronted, in the midst of their incredibly busy and demanding lives, with such issues as injustice, racism, and discrimination. How do Notre Dame graduates create communion with God when they are confronted by a worldly emphasis on monetary gain and social status? When they see others being subjected to great poverty and their human rights disregarded? When they watch children struggle to learn in under-resourced or ineffective schools? These obstacles confront all of us in our daily lives, often drawing us away from God and prayer when we are most in need of grace.

This selection of prayers and devotions reminds us of the many and always-beautiful opportunities we have had for prayer at Notre Dame. Whether it be quiet, individual reflection at the Grotto, small community Mass in the intimate friendship of the dorm, or the gathering of the entire Notre Dame family at the Basilica of the Sacred Heart, Notre Dame students have always strived to strengthen their relationship with God. We remember

times spent in communion with others—engaging with the intellectual dilemmas of our day in the classroom, helping the marginalized through activities of service, enjoying the gift of leisure with one another at the dining hall or on our teams' sport fields. In all these sacred places on the Notre Dame campus, we have felt God's intimate presence—within ourselves, our activities, our relationships with others.

This *Notre Dame Book* of Prayer offers us a way to rediscover those sacred spaces, in the midst of our daily lives, wherever God has called us, where we can be filled with the knowledge of God in every minute, no matter how insignificant or momentous the time may appear to us. With memories of the sacred spaces of our beloved Notre Dame campus as a touchstone, our desire to pray is renewed, despite ever-present obstacles. We recall perhaps the greatest lesson that our time beneath Our Lady's Dome taught us, that the places and people of our everyday lives are filled with God's response to our request, "Lord, teach us to pray." May Notre Dame Our Mother—Mary, the Mother of God—always nourish within each of us the deepest thirst to remain close to her Son Jesus through our lives of prayer. May this *Notre Dame Book of Prayer* keep us connected to Notre Dame and, through her, to her Son.

Theodore M. Hesburgh, C.S.C.
President Emeritus of the University of Notre Dame

✠ INTRODUCTION ✠

I am delighted to offer *The Notre Dame Book of Prayer*, a joint effort between Ave Maria Press and Campus Ministry at Notre Dame.

For over one hundred years, Campus Ministry has offered prayer books to incoming first-year students. In recent years, these books have emphasized not only traditional and seasonal prayers, but also prayers written by members of the Notre Dame family, prayers for special moments and occasions, and prayers written to underscore a special place on campus that lifts one's heart and mind to God.

The Notre Dame Book of Prayer is our attempt to extend this same opportunity to the broader Notre Dame community, as well as to our friends and the many people for whom Notre Dame is a special place, even a living symbol of our Catholic faith's deep aspirations. It is often true that in a world and society of shifting cultural values, Notre Dame is rare solid ground!

I hope that this book of prayers will be a source of inspiration that brings together traditional and liturgical prayer with personal reflections often based on the many places that for each of us represent the best of Notre Dame spirituality in the Holy Cross tradition.

Blessed Basile Moreau, C.S.C., founder of the Congregation of Holy Cross, was inspired to found a religious community that included priests, brothers, and sisters, whose special and particular patrons mirrored the Holy Family itself. And he was favored with developing an educational vision that included both the mind and heart. One of his first disciples, Father Edward Sorin, C.S.C., gave flesh to this vision that, in the words of Professor Edward Fisher, has been a long descending blessing for generations of Notre Dame students, faculty, staff, parents, and alumni—as well as for countless friends.

May Notre Dame continue to inspire and encourage many future generations to share such a challenging and realizable goal!

Richard V. Warner, C.S.C.
Director, Campus Ministry

We Are ND

Lord, we thank you for the blessing
of belonging to the Notre Dame family.
Whether as students or alumni, faculty or staff,
parents or friends of Our Lady's university,
we are ND.
What a gift this is!

Help us to live the calling
that comes with this gift:
the call to excellence,
the call to service,
the call to faith,
the call to integrity,
the call to humility.
Help us to be different
and to make a difference.
Allow us to bravely meet the challenges
we may face when we are
caring for others.

Give us the grace to be more like Mary, our Mother:
tender, strong, and true.
Increase in our hearts love for Notre Dame
and the desire to be her faithful sons and daughters.

Chuck Lennon, '61, '62 MA
Executive Director, Notre Dame Alumni Association

BEST-LOVED PRAYERS

✠ ✠

Our Father

Our Father, who art in heaven,
hallowed be thy name;
thy kingdom come;
thy will be done, on earth as it is in heaven.
Give us this day our daily bread;
and forgive us our trespasses
as we forgive those who trespass against us;
and lead us not into temptation,
but deliver us from evil. Amen.

Hail Mary

Hail Mary,
full of grace,
the Lord is with thee.
Blessed art thou among women,
and blessed is the fruit
of thy womb, Jesus.
Holy Mary,
Mother of God,
pray for us sinners now
and at the hour of death. Amen.

Glory Be

Glory be to the Father, and to the Son,
   and to the Holy Spirit,
as it was in the beginning, is now,
and will be for ever. Amen.

1

IN THE BEGINNING

Prayers for New Beginnings

✣ THE GROTTO ✣

How naturally your campus surrounds this cove of trees and rock; how affectionately nonchalant your welcome is, and how reflexive my response. When I kneel, or sit, or stand, or stroll by your quiet candled cave, the fractures of my life and self and soul become all the more acute. How peevish, whining, and selfish my prayer must sound to you, as I light a candle to mark the begging of some favor.

But being here emboldens me, because I know whose mother you are; because I have a mother, too, and I know what it is to be a mother's son. In your kind company I am again and again reminded of how almost preposterous it is that he loves the likes of me; that even such meanness, cowardice, and arrogance as my own could not prevent him from wanting to take on the human flesh I share with him, to be so much like me, like some guy, like some mother's son.

How even more amazed you must be, to be his mother. To love him as my mother loves me, and to be loved by him as I love her. The distinctly domestic glow of your mutual love draws us here with all sorts of prayers, from paltry thanksgivings to anguished appeals. Here we can pause and share a bit of that love in which all your titles—Mother of God, Queen of Heaven, Seat of Wisdom, Our Lady, Notre Dame—coalesce, allowing us to address you as he himself does, Mother.

Michael Garvey, '74
Office of Public Affairs and Communication

✢ BEGINNING TO PRAY ✢

Beginning to pray may well have something to do with how one was introduced to prayer.

In grammar school, the Benedictine sisters taught me to say: "Divine Infant of Bethlehem, come and take birth in my heart" some six thousand times during Advent (that being the number of years since creation in the Garden of Eden). I still say that prayer to this day as I walk along the sidewalks of the Notre Dame campus. Walking time is prayer time. So are red lights, elevator waits, even three identical digits on the digital clock. I often make the Sign of the Cross whenever I become aware of one of the million ways our lives could be endangered, given all the things within us and around us that can go wrong and often do.

In high school, Benedictine monks encouraged me to compose my own prayer. It was revelatory of the trials and fears of an adolescent young man: "Saint Agnes, virgin martyr, who loved her purity above all else, help me preserve mine; who suffered terrible tortures for the love of God, increase my love; and who suffered martyrdom, strengthen me in time of persecution." I still say that prayer.

On to Notre Dame in the early 1950s, where morning inspection in the residence hall was followed by Mass—unless you turned around and went back to bed, the resident priest watching you scorn the grace of God. I went to Mass.

It was at Old College in my second semester that I was introduced to regular morning and evening prayer. Joining the Congregation of Holy Cross led me to a novitiate year in swampland around Jordan, Minnesota. I learned to write a prayer journal, and writing became a form of praying.

Amidst life's competing demands, I now find early morning is my best prayer time. I love rocking on Sorin Hall's porch waiting for sunrise, with a cup of coffee sweetened with awe and delight in my Creator. I have by now become well aware of my need for and happiness with contemplative prayer—prayer greatly assisted by the right place and the right time. I ask for my next breath, that I know I cannot draw without God's constant assistance. I know what matters is not what I do, but what God is doing. Why anything? Why me? I can sit with that every morning and never grow weary of the wonder of it all.

I wish evening prayer would go better than it does. I find myself tired out at the end of the day and prayer is more difficult. I want to be thankful, and I know gratitude is the secret of any happy life. I believe God knows what we need and loves us, so our evening prayer need not inform God of what is going on in the world or plead with God to take care of us. Evening prayer can be simple. "Thank you for taking care of all this. I know you are. Goodnight!"

Prayer is never my initiative. It is always a response to a prior invitation that turns my mind and heart to God. We must receive before we can give. We must breathe in before we breathe out.

Prayer is an exchange with God. Prayer is attending to what God is doing within us and in the world. Prayer is the recognition that we are but a speck of stardust upon a speck of a planet in a galaxy, itself but a speck in an expanding universe. Our prayer is silent in the big scheme of things, but remains close to the heart of God. The God who wanted nothing so much as to be one of us in the flesh and to love us even unto death.

Prayer is listening to the silence in our hearts, and beginning to pray is a willingness to take our next breath in exchange with God, who is more part of us than we are part of ourselves. Beginning to pray is the beginning of the greatest adventure on earth.

Nicholas Ayo, C.S.C.
Professor Emeritus of Liberal Studies

PRAYERS FOR NEW BEGINNINGS

See, I am making all things new.
—Revelation 21:5

We are always beginning again: new relationships, new homes, new experiences. The crux of our Christian faith—the resurrection—teaches us that new life always follows death. Whether literal or figurative, new life also calls for blessing. These prayers express gratitude for all the newness of life and ask for God's presence as we undertake new ventures, make new commitments, and begin new journeys.

I Tremble on the Edge of a Maybe

O God of beginnings,
as your Spirit moved
over the face of the deep
on the first day of creation,
move with me now

in my time of beginnings,
when the air is rain-washed,
the bloom is on the bush,
and the world seems fresh
and full of possibilities,
and I feel ready and full.
I tremble on the edge of a maybe,
a first time,
a new thing,
a tentative start,
and the wonder of it lays its fingers on my lips.

In silence, Lord,
I share now my eagerness
and my uneasiness
about this something different
I would be or do;
and I listen for your leading
to help me separate the light
from the darkness
in the change I seek to shape
and which is shaping me.
　　　　Ted Loder

Prayer for the Spiritual Journey

God of life,
give us a vision of our earthly journey.
Guide us on our pilgrimage through this world.
Be our constant companion as we find our way.
Help us when we get lost.
Strengthen us in times of fear.
Grant us the courage to cross the borders that divide
and break down the walls that exclude.

May we offer a welcome to all,
especially our neighbor in need.
And at the end of our sojourn,
as we cross the border of death,
lead us to our true homeland,
where we hope to know at last your eternal embrace
and be united as one body in Christ.

Daniel G. Groody, C.S.C.
Center for Latino Spirituality and Culture

Prayer for the First Day of the Year

Eternal and Almighty God, who makes all things new,
we thank you that today you have allowed us to begin a new
    year.
Here in your presence we make our resolutions for the days to
    come.

We resolve to be faithful and true to those who love us,
and loyal to those who are our friends,
so that we may never bring worry to their minds or distress to
    their hearts.

We resolve to live in forgiveness and in kindness,
that, like Jesus, we may go about always doing good.

We resolve to live in diligence and effort,
that we may use the full gifts and the talents that God has given
    us.

We resolve to live in goodness and purity,
that we ourselves may resist temptation,
and that we may be a strength to others who are tempted.

We resolve to live in sympathy and in gentleness,
that we may bring comfort to the sorrowing
and understanding to those who are confused.

We resolve to live in serenity and in self-control,
that no anger or passion may disturb our own peace nor the
    peace of others.

We resolve to show our love for God by keeping his
    Commandments
and ask Jesus to bless us with his peace and joy for doing this.

O God, our Loving Father,
you have given us the grace to make our own resolutions,
grant us also the strength to keep them through the coming year.

> St. Peter, Prince of the Apostles Catholic Church
> Corpus Christi, Texas

*A college degree is not a sign that one is a finished
product, but an indication a person is prepared for life.*

> Edward A. "Monk" Malloy, C.S.C.
> President Emeritus of the University of Notre Dame

 ## New Year's Prayer for World Day of Peace

May Mary help us discover the face of Jesus, Prince of Peace.
May she support and accompany us in this new year;
may she obtain for us and for the whole world
the desired gift of peace!
So be it!

> Pope John Paul II

Epiphany House Blessing

Use chalk to mark the entrance with the current year and the inscription "CMB," the initials of Caspar, Melchior, and Balthasar, the traditional names of the magi. It also stands for the Latin phrase Christus Mansionem Benedicat, *which means "Christ, bless this home."*

Lord God of heaven and earth,
you revealed your only begotten Son
to every nation by the guidance of a star.
Bless this house and all who inhabit it.
May we be blessed with health, goodness of heart,
gentleness, and the keeping of your law.
Fill us with the light of Christ,
that our love for each other may go out to all.
We ask this through Christ our Lord.
   Roman Ritual

Prayer for Justice as the School Year Begins

God of Hope,
vibrant colors of your creation
remind us that all we have is gift from you.

When our world is at unrest,
ruptured by violence and distrust,
you shower us with gifts
to seek, to discover, to guide, and to learn.

Open our hearts to recognize your presence in our midst.
Enable us to be people of hospitality,
trusting that with your grace new life will sprout.

Grant us the strength and wisdom
to overcome fear that limits the action of your Spirit.
And may your Spirit impel us to act justly
in all that we do.

    Judith R. Fean, '84 MA
    Campus Ministry, Saint Mary's College

Prayer for Retirement

Good and gracious God,
I am grateful to you for so many blessings,
some acknowledged, many unrecognized.
It has definitely been "push and shove" on your part at times.
As a friend of mine says,
"God always pushes us where he wants us to go."

And, so you have. And, so you shall.
Here we are, at this next juncture:
"determining what I want to do with the second half of my life,"
as another friend says.
Retirement does not seem to be realistic.
There is much more that can and should be done.

There are so many possibilities to serve you by serving others.
Dear Lord, you have blessed me with many talents,
and definitely guided me along the way so far.
My prayer today and all days
is that you will "push and shove" me
where you want me to go during these "retirement years."

    Joseph P. Mulligan, '59

Engagement Blessing

May God be with you and bless you.
May you see your children's children.
May you be poor in misfortune, rich in blessings.
May you know nothing but happiness
from this day forward.

Traditional Irish Blessing

*Holy Cross will grow like a mighty tree and
constantly shoot forth new limbs and new
branches which will be nourished by the same
sap and endowed with the same life.*

Blessed Basile Moreau, C.S.C.
Founder of the Congregation of Holy Cross

Prayer by an Engaged Couple

May our love increasingly be a sign of Christ's love for the
    Church.
Let our daily nurturing of our relationship use the Mass as a
    model.

Let us each day humbly acknowledge our faults
and ask for forgiveness for any hurts we have caused the other.
May we take any opportunity for praising and affirming
    the talents and efforts of the other.
May we offer our time, understanding, and active, empathetic
    listening
even when we judge that we have heard before what we are
    hearing now.
May we pray with and for each other in whatever ways we can.

May we try to build a solid foundation
of openness and trust based upon similar values.

May we celebrate our coming vows
and put the stress on our relationship building,
not on the wedding day details that will soon pale in importance.

May we treat each other with a sacred trust that seeks to build
    up.
Help us believe that God sends us forth as a couple
to become an ever clearer channel of his love.
Don't let us neglect to give each other a kiss of peace often!
May we go in peace to love and serve the Lord.
> <u>Kathy and Kevin Misiewicz</u>
> <u>Mendoza College of Business</u>

Prayer for Expectant Parents

This prayer is especially fitting when a pregnancy seems difficult. The opening and closing are recited together, then each parent prays his or her part in turn.

Together: Thank you for blessing us with this pregnancy. We know it is a gift. But as our baby's birth approaches, it seems more difficult to feel the excitement, joy, love, and gratitude we felt when we first learned we would become parents; when we first heard our baby's heartbeat; when we first saw our baby move and turn in grainy ultrasound images.

Mother: I feel exhausted from waking up so often at night. Give me strength to handle the chores and demands that still face me each day.

Father: I feel bothered because my wife cannot do the tasks and chores she usually does. Give me patience to handle my added responsibilities without complaint or resentment.

Mother: I feel uncomfortable and in pain from the additional weight and strain of pregnancy. Grant me the resolve to endure the continuing changes in my body as our baby grows inside me.

Father: I feel helpless to relieve my wife's discomfort and pain. Grant me empathy so I can better understand how I can help her endure the final weeks and days of her pregnancy.

Mother: I feel worried my relationship with my husband [and my other child(ren)] may change after our baby is born. Allow me to savor each of my relationships as the birth approaches.

Father: I feel concerned that my wife and I will not be as close after our baby is born. Allow me to cherish the time we spend together now as the birth approaches.

Mother: I feel afraid that our baby will not be healthy and that I will suffer complications during delivery. Guide those who will deliver our baby and care for me and help me to trust their skills, knowledge, and compassion.

Father: I feel afraid that my wife or our baby will be injured during delivery. Guide those who will deliver our baby and care for my wife and help me to trust their skills, knowledge, and compassion.

Together: Please help us move past these feelings of fear, worry, sadness, helplessness, discomfort, bother, and exhaustion. Help us to focus instead on our excitement and joy for the new life that will join our family soon; on our love for one another, [for our other child(ren),] and for our growing baby; and on our gratitude for this gift of becoming parents.

Brian '94, '99 and Kristi '93 Kubicki

Blessing of a New Baby

Lord Jesus Christ, Son of the living God,
you were begotten before all time,
and yet desired to become an infant in time.
You are delighted with the innocence of tender years.
You lovingly embraced the children who were brought to you,
and blessed them.
In the blessings of your sweetness,
go before this infant and grant that no evil may mar his/her
    intellect.
Grant too that, growing in age, wisdom, and grace,
he/she may ever be pleasing to you,
who live and are King and God with God the Father
in the unity of the Holy Spirit, for ever and ever.
    Roman Ritual

Prayer for Those Adopting a Child

We have waited for so long
for this child of choice.

Bless us with an abundance of your love
that we may be good parents,
that we may create a home of blessing,
that we may encourage this child
to the fullness of his/her potential.
Bless our child, O God.
Give her security in our family,
the joy of laughter in our home,
and the courage to face
the challenges ahead.
Let our child know the love

we feel so deeply for her,
and let this love be a strength
to confront the opportunities of life.
>Vienna Cobb Anderson

Prayer for a New Grandchild

Bless, I pray, this beautiful child,
so newly come into our family.
I thank thee for the wonder and privilege
of looking for the first time in the tiny face of our child's child.
We anticipate his/her first smiles, first words, first steps,
and pray that he/she may flourish in a climate of affection.
May we be a loving link for him/her with an earlier generation.
I pray that he/she may grow up into a peaceful world
where he/she may realize all his/her potential,
maturing from a happy childhood
to a life of accomplishment and service.
>Josephine Robertson

Blessing of a New Pet

Most high, almighty Lord, our Creator,
yours are the praise, the glory, the honor and all blessings!
To you alone do all things belong.
Be praised for giving us
the animals, birds and fish which fill your world.
May we think of you and thank you
when we play with and care for our pets.
Be praised for making us so happy to have our pets
and to have them to play with.
We ask you, Lord, that we may be good to our pets always,

so that they may be happy also.
Help us always to take care of them
so that they will be healthy.

Name of pet, may you be blessed
in the name of God who created you,
and may you and *name of owner*
enjoy life together with our God.
    → Thomas Simons
    → Adapted by Robert Morrison and Richard J. Fairchild

Prayer before Starting on a Journey

My holy Angel Guardian,
ask the Lord to bless the journey which I undertake,
that it may profit the health of my soul and body;
that I may reach its end,
and that, returning safe and sound,
I may find my family in good health.
Do thou guard, guide, and preserve us.

Runner's Prayer before Beginning a Race

Almighty and ever-living God,
As I prepare to embark on the journey ahead,
be my strength for that journey.
Help me to remember that each journey
begins with a single step.
When the road becomes sparse and my will begins to wane,
help me to recognize that you will never leave my side.
May each leg of the race emblazon my desire and zeal
to be a beacon of Christ's light

in a world that can seem at times covered in darkness.
My talents are not my own, all I am belongs to you.
May I never forget that all I have is on loan;
I am to use what I am given
to accomplish your will on earth.
Allow me Lord to use my talents
to be a sign of hope in the world.
May the road rise up to meet me,
may the wind always be at my back,
and may the sun shine warmly upon my face.
Come Holy Spirit, be the force behind my stride.
I pray this in Christ's name always
and through the intercession of Notre Dame, Our Mother.

Michael S. Suso
Alliance for Catholic Education

Prayer for Openness to New Experiences

Lord, take me where you want me to go,
let me meet who you want me to meet,
tell me what you want me to say,
and keep me out of your way.

Mychal Judge, O.F.M.

Prayer for a New Attitude

Give me a pure heart—that I may see thee,
A humble heart—that I may hear thee,
A heart of love—that I may serve thee,
A heart of faith—that I may abide in thee.

Dag Hammarskjöld

2

OF THE HOURS

Prayers for Everyday

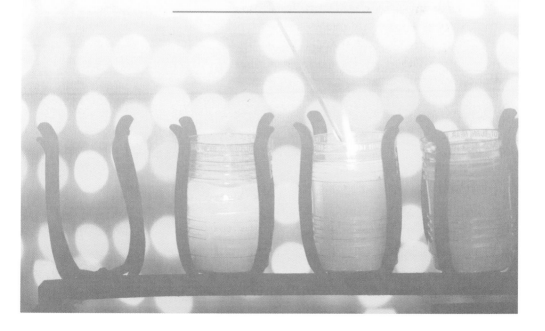

✦ THE DORMS ✦

A knock at the door, the click of a lock, the clomping of shoes coming down the stairs, the silence of the chapel, the laughter of section mates hanging out in the hall. The residence halls at the University of Notre Dame are more than the four walls and a roof that provide shelter; they are our homes.

Each hall is unique, yet this experience of living in community links us with fellow Domers, past and present. The laughter and the tears, the long nights of studying and the dreaded trips to class in the freezing cold build solidarity, but also can be moments filled with grace.

The experience of God's loving presence is found within these halls in the most tangible and intangible ways. We gather together on Sunday nights to listen to scripture and break the bread that nourishes us and gives us life. Yet that is just the beginning of the experience of God in our residential life. It is in the most ordinary moments that God is found. The listening ear of a good friend or the offer of help from a person down the hall is the often-unnoticed, yet profound experience of the divine.

So whether you live or lived in South Quad or North Quad, God Quad, West Quad, Mod Quad, FOG, University Village, or even Carroll Hall, you have been privileged to share in something only a few have had the chance to do: experience God's love in a home under the Dome.

Cynthia Broderick, O.P.
Rector, Pasquerilla East Hall

✤ KEEPING THE HOURS ✤

People sometimes associate the word *liturgical* with formality, repetition, and being a trifle boring. If that were the case, then *liturgical prayer* would mean prayer that is not meaningful and personal by being spontaneous, but prayer that is rote and tedious because it is out of a book.

Nothing could be further from a proper understanding of the Liturgy of the Hours.

I learned this in theory first, but in practice later. All through graduate school I read about liturgical prayer, but it was not until my family and I were received into the Catholic Church that its full reality became apparent. People born Catholic are cradle Catholics, but I refer to myself as a *credo* Catholic because it was the theological truths that drew me in.

And the most profound truth I experienced was the sense of being part of a mystical body. It doesn't just include the people in one particular parish; rather, it stretches around the globe and back to the apostles. This is the Church with whom I pray the Liturgy of the Hours.

The source of liturgy is the Father reaching out in love through Christ to sanctify his creation. The return flow of thanksgiving, gathered up in Christ and returned to the Father, is accomplished in our hearts through the operation of the Holy Spirit. Liturgical life is being incorporated into the life of the Trinity. By means of the Holy Spirit, we become by grace what Christ is by nature, and share his relationship to God the Father.

This is what happens in liturgical prayer. It occurs within this cycle of love. My private prayer is spontaneous, centered upon a need that I experience individually; but liturgical prayer is held in common with each other, the angels, and the saints in heaven. It is given and received, not invented or altered.

This is why living under the discipline of this liturgy was emphasized so strongly by the Second Vatican Council, although it has gone largely unnoticed in the reform that has unfolded since. The Constitution on the Sacred Liturgy summarizes this by saying that Christ brought heaven's song to earth, and earth's prayer to heaven:

> Christ Jesus, high priest of the new and eternal covenant, taking human nature, introduced into this earthly exile that hymn which is sung throughout all ages in the halls of heaven. He joins the entire community of mankind to himself, associating it with his own singing of this canticle of divine praise. For he continues his priestly work through the agency of his Church, which is ceaselessly engaged in praising the Lord and interceding for the salvation of the whole world. She does this, not only by celebrating the Eucharist, but also in other ways, especially by praying the divine office. (par 83)

Praying the hours is participation in the ongoing work of Christ, and a premier way that the laity exercise their baptismal priesthood.

In the early church, *all* Christians paused for prayer during the day, not just priests and religious. All the baptized faithful punctuated their day with prayer. The morning and evening hours are especially important, as they put parentheses around each day. At dawn we place our activities into the hands of God, and at dusk we offer thanks for blessings bestowed and beg forgiveness for wrongs committed. Bedtime (compline) is an opportunity to give our souls repose in God, a rehearsal for the day when we will be called to do so finally, at our death. We are attuned to the seasons of the liturgical year in the cycle of readings; the Psalms train our hearts in pious emotions; under this discipline we give thanks even when we don't feel like it, and we petition for people and causes we would otherwise forget. This is the advantage of

structured prayer—it has a foundation and is not blown around by our temporary moods.

The public prayer of the Church is a different kind of praying than my private prayer. I am still embracing this privilege with the fullness that the Council intended. I am hopeful that individuals, families, communities of devotion, and parishes will find ways to restore this gift to our generation. The Liturgy of the Hours is the prayer of the church passing through our lips.

David W. Fagerberg
Center for Liturgy

PRAYERS FOR EVERYDAY

✛   ✛

This is the day that the Lord has made;
let us rejoice and be glad in it.
—Psalm 118:24

Every Sunday evening, students and other Notre Dame folks gather in the basilica for Vespers, the traditional evening prayer that is part of the Liturgy of the Hours. For many, it helps put closure on the weekend and ready them for the next week of classes. Once seen as only for priests and monastics, the Liturgy of the Hours—or the Divine Office, as it is sometimes called—is increasingly being adopted by laypeople who appreciate the rhythm of praying regularly with others around the world. Even if you don't get up at dawn for lauds, morning and evening prayers are the perfect way to begin and end your day.

St. Brigid of Kildare's Prayer

I arise today
through a mighty strength:
God's power to guide me,
God's might to uphold me,
God's eyes to watch over me,
God's ear to hear me,
God's word to give me speech,
God's hand to guard me,
God's way to lie before me,
God's shield to shelter me,
God's host to secure me.

It is not merely we who pray, but his Spirit who prays in us. And we who busy ourselves in announcing the Lord's kingdom need to come back often enough and sit at his feet and listen still more closely.

**Constitution Three
of the Congregation of Holy Cross**

Christ Our Morning Star

O Christ, our Morning Star,
Splendor of Light Eternal,
shining with the glory of the rainbow,
come and waken us
from the grayness of our apathy,
and renew in us your gift of hope.

St. Bede the Venerable

Simple Morning Prayer

Blessed be you, God,
for creating me.
St. Clare

Child's Morning Prayer

Dear God,
we give you this day all of our work,
all of our play,
all that we do and all that we say.

Mother's Morning Prayer

God our Father, in your loving providence
you send your holy angels to watch over us.
Hear my prayer and surround my family always with their
    protection.
Keep my children safe from all harm.
St. Michael, St. Raphael, St. Gabriel,
help them to be aware of God's presence throughout their day.
St. Michael, defend them against any evil that seeks to come
    against them.
St. Raphael, heal their mind and spirit from all doubt.
Be their companion and grant them safe journeys wherever they
    go.
St. Gabriel, guide them should they stray from their soul's
    pathway.
I ask this all in the name of Jesus.
Margaret Gloster
University of Notre Dame Press

Teach My Heart Today

O Lord my God,
teach my heart today where to see you,
how to see you,
where and how to find you.
You have made me and remade me,
and you have given me all the good things I
have ever possessed—
and still I do not know you.

Teach me to seek you,
for I cannot seek you unless you teach me,
or find you unless you reveal yourself to me.
Help me to seek you in desire,
help me desire you in my seeking,
help me to find you by loving you,
help me to love you when I find you.

Mary Ford-Grabowsky

Morning Offering

O Jesus,
through the Immaculate Heart of Mary,
I offer you my prayers, works,
joys, and sufferings
of this day for all the intentions
of your Sacred Heart,
in union with the Holy Sacrifice of the Mass
throughout the world,
in reparation for my sins,

for the intentions of all my relatives and friends,
and in particular
for the intentions of the Holy Father.
The Apostleship of Prayer

Morning Prayer I

O my God! I offer thee all my actions of this day
for the intentions and for the glory
of the Sacred Heart of Jesus.
I desire to sanctify every beat of my heart,
my every thought, my simplest works,
by uniting them to its infinite merits;
and I wish to make reparation for my sins
by casting them into the furnace of its Merciful Love.

O my God! I ask of thee
for myself and for those whom I hold dear,
the grace to fulfill perfectly thy Holy Will,
to accept for love of thee
the joys and sorrows of this passing life,
so that we may one day be united together
in heaven for all Eternity.
St. Thérèse of Lisieux

Morning Prayer II

Lord God Almighty,
who hast safely brought us to the beginning of this day,
defend us in the same by thy mighty power,
that this day we may fall into no sin,
but that all our words may so proceed,

and all our thoughts and actions may be so directed
as to do always that which is just in thy sight.

Roman Breviary

Shine through Me

Jesus, shine through me
and be so in me that every person I come in contact with
may feel your presence in my soul.

John Henry Newman

Canticle of Zechariah (*Benedictus*)

(recited or sung as part of Lauds or Morning Prayer)

Blessed be the Lord, the God of Israel;
he has come to his people and set them free.
He has raised up for us a mighty savior,
born of the house of his servant David.

Through his holy prophets he promised of old
that he would save us from our enemies,
from the hands of all who hate us.

He promised to show mercy to our fathers
and to remember his holy covenant.

This was the oath he swore to our father Abraham:
to set us free from the hands of our enemies,
free to worship him without fear,
holy and righteous in his sight
all the days of our life.

You, my child shall be called the prophet of the Most High,
for you will go before the Lord to prepare his way,
to give his people knowledge of salvation
by the forgiveness of their sins.

In the tender compassion of our God
the dawn from on high shall break upon us,
to shine on those who dwell in darkness and the shadow of
    death,
and to guide our feet into the way of peace.

Liturgy of the Hours

*With the eyes of faith consider the greatness
of the mission and the wonderful amount
of good that one can accomplish.*

Blessed Basile Moreau, C.S.C.
Founder of the Congregation of Holy Cross

Daily Prayer

O God, help me strive with all my might
to become humble and pure of heart,
without which it is impossible
to truly know you and serve you.
Open my eyes and ears to learn
from the holiness and wisdom
of your saints in other religions.
Do not let me forget the poor.

Bradley Malkovsky
Department of Theology

Midday Prayer

Teach us, dear Lord, to number our days;
that we may apply our hearts unto wisdom.
Oh, satisfy us early with thy mercy,
that we may rejoice and be glad all of our days.
And let the beauty of the Lord our God be upon us;
and establish thou the work of our hands.
And let the beauty of the Lord our God be upon us;
and establish thou the work of our hands, dear Lord.

Northumbria Community, Ireland

*If during prayer, you do nothing but bring your
heart from distraction again and again into God's
presence though it went away every time you brought
it back, your time would be very well spent.*

St. Francis de Sales

Noon Prayer

Lord Jesus Christ,
at noon, when darkness covered all the earth,
you mounted the wood of the cross
as the innocent victim for our redemption.
May your light be always with us,
to guide us to eternal life in that kingdom
where you live and reign for ever and ever.

Liturgy of the Hours

⊹ ———————————————————

(recited twice daily, in the morning and evening)

Hear, O Israel!
The Lord our God is Lord alone!
You shall love the Lord your God with all your heart,
with all your soul,
with all your mind,
and with all your strength.

Evening Prayer I

O Lord my God,
thank you for bringing this day to a close.
Thank you for giving me rest in body and soul.
Your hand has been over me
and has guarded and preserved me.
Forgive my lack of faith
and any wrong that I have done today,
and help me to forgive all who have wronged me.

Let me sleep in peace under your protection,
and keep me from all the temptations of darkness.
Into your hands I commend my loved ones.
I commend to you my body and soul.
O God, your holy name be praised.
Dietrich Bonhoeffer

Evening Prayer II

May God support us all the day long
till the shadows lengthen
and the evening comes
and the busy world is hushed
and the fever of life is over
and our work is done.
Then in mercy
may God give us a safe lodging
and a holy rest
and peace at the last.

John Henry Newman

O Radiant Light

O radiant light, O sun divine
of God the Father's deathless face,
O image of the light sublime
that fills the heav'nly dwelling place.

Lord Jesus Christ, as daylight fades,
as shine the lights of eventide,
we praise the Father with the Son,
the Spirit blest and with them one.

O Son of God, the source of life,
praise is your due by night and day;
unsullied lips must raise the strain
of your proclaimed and splendid name.

Translated by William G. Storey
Professor Emeritus of Liturgy

Canticle of Mary (*Magnificat*)

(recited or sung as part of Vespers or Evening Prayer)

My soul proclaims the greatness of the Lord,
my spirit rejoices in God my Savior
for he has looked with favor on his lowly servant.

From this day all generations will call me blessed:
the Almighty has done great things for me,
and holy is his Name.

He has mercy on those who fear him
in every generation.

He has shown the strength of his arm,
He has scattered the proud in their conceit.

He has cast down the mighty from their thrones,
and has lifted up the lowly.

He has filled the hungry with good things,
and the rich he has sent away empty.

He has come to the help of his servant Israel
for he has remembered his promise of mercy,
the promise he made to our fathers,
to Abraham and his children for ever.

Liturgy of the Hours

Children's Bedtime Prayers

Angel of God
my guardian dear
to whom God's love
commits me here.
Ever this day
be at my side
to light, to guard, to rule, to guide.

* * *

Now I lay me down to sleep,
I pray the Lord my soul to keep.
if I should die before I wake,
I pray the Lord my soul to take.

Child's Evening Prayer

Bless me, God, the long night through,
and bless my mommy and daddy, too,
and everyone who needs your care,
make tomorrow bright and fair,
and thank you, God, I humbly pray,
for all you did for me today.

J. P. McEvoy

Night Prayer I

Protect us, Lord, as we stay awake;
watch over us as we sleep,
that awake, we may keep watch with Christ,
and asleep, rest in his peace.

Liturgy of the Hours

Night Prayer II

Watch thou, dear Lord,
with those who wake, or watch, or weep tonight,
and give thine angels charge over those who sleep.
Tend thy sick ones, Lord Christ.
Rest thy weary ones.
Bless thy dying ones.
Soothe thy suffering ones.
Pity thine afflicted ones.
Shield thy joyous ones.
And all, for thy love's sake.

St. Augustine

Lord, one more day to love you!

Charles de Foucauld

Canticle of Simeon (*Nunc Dimittis*)

(recited or sung as part of Compline or Night Prayer)

Lord, now you let your servant go in peace;
your word has been fulfilled:
my own eyes have seen the salvation
which you have prepared in the sight of every people:
a light to reveal you to the nations
and the glory of your people, Israel.

Liturgy of the Hours

During a Sleepless Night

Lord, I cannot sleep. I lie awake, thinking about things and
worrying.
I worry about my health, my family, the future—a countless
number of things.
I am weary but find no rest.
I remember your words:
"Can any of you by worrying add a single hour to your span of
life?" (Mt 6:27).
Help me to take your words to heart, O Lord.
Let me place each concern in your hands.
Grant me peace, O Lord, and let me sleep.

Robert M. Hamma, '83 MA

*I am so sorely in need of prayer! In it
rests all my hope and consolation.*

Blessed Basile Moreau, C.S.C.
Founder of the Congregation of Holy Cross

The Jesuit Examination of Conscience

Thanksgiving
Lord, I realize that all, even myself, is a gift from you.
(Today, for what things am I most grateful?)

Intention
Lord, open my eyes and ears to be more honest with myself.
(Today, what do I really want for myself?)

Examination
Lord, show me what has been happening to me and in me
this day.
(Today, in what ways have I experienced your love?)

Contrition
Lord, I am still learning to grow in your love.
(Today, what choices have been inadequate responses to
your love?)

Hope
Lord, let me look with longing toward the future.
(Today, how will I let you lead me to a brighter tomorrow?)

3

BLESS US, O LORD

Prayers for Meals and Family Experiences

✤ SOUTH DINING HALL ✤

We sittin' right-right or left-left?" To onlookers, this might have sounded like a tired political debate, but to many Notre Dame undergrads, it meant the difference between a good meal at South Dining Hall and a lonely one. Sure, we went there for our favorite stir-fry dish, latest panini creation, or the unlimited cereal buffet, but we also went with a hunger decidedly deeper and more insatiable than that for which our taste buds longed. We need only recall the anxiety we felt when we lost our friends amidst the vast sea of diners to recognize that we craved much more than our abundantly filled trays could satisfy.

Oh, if those faithful troops of ready tables and chairs, wise and weathered witnesses to years of human hunger, could tell their tales of all we brought to their ranks . . . heaping helpings of heartbreaks and breakthroughs; last-minute cramming and endless laughing fits; fall break insights and spring break slip-ups; weekend anecdotes and daily dining-hall crushes; generous sides of fear and goodness, topped with ripe insecurity, and finished with refreshing hints of faith and hope; all hold the rich vulnerability and unpalatable trust.

Every Sunday brunch, I sat right-right with the other members of the Folk Choir at the raised head table, under the gaze of the Last Supper mural. What did that sacred table above have to do with our messy one below? Absolutely everything, if only we could have taken it in, the way we did our "Yo Cream" with sprinkles.

→ Colleen Moore, '97, '04 MDiv
Center for Catechetical Initiatives

FATHER, SON,
SPIRIT, HOLY

Dinner hour, and I sit down to table with my wife and three small children, ready to talk turkey. Today it is my youngest son's turn for grace, and he starts us off with the Sign of the Cross. He has a unique take on this act, as in so many other aspects of his life: not unlike a third-base coach, he makes a flurry of motions, touching forehead, belly, shoulders, nose, temples, ears, and (finally) tongue, all the while chanting, at a terrific pace, Father, Son, Spirit, Holy.

As usual, he sends his family into stitches, and after a while we bring him around to a slightly more orthodox Sign of the Cross, but as his mother and sister and brother recover from the giggles and set to work eating their meals, his father's mind, as usual, rambles. Whence came this unusual motion of the hand, and incantation? Why do we mark moments great and small, holy and horrendous, with this gentle hand-made echo of the crucifix? Father, Son, Holy Ghost, I whispered as a boy, and Father, Son, Holy Spirit, I whisper as a man, in moments of joy and fear, prayer and penitence, before a meal, during the Mass, after a death. I make the Sign of the Cross in wonder, when my children do or say something that slaps me into remembering they came to me from the hand of the Lord. I make the sign in gratitude when they finally fall asleep. I make it in desperate prayer when they are wan and weak and sick. I make it before meals, during Masses, after funerals, after baptisms; I make it in awe and epiphany and tragedy.

Scholars trace the practice as far back as the year 110, by which time it was already established as a common gesture among

Christians. Those early Christians honored, in a simple physical gesture, the geometric shape on which Christ gave his life for us. It is a small miracle, perhaps, that this gesture has persisted unchanged throughout many nations and centuries; but then again miracles are not unusual, are they?

Such a simple act, our hands cutting the air like the wings of birds, fingers alighting gently on our bodies in memory of the body broken for us.

Father, we say, touching our heads, the seats of our cerebrations, and we think of the Maker, that vast incomprehensible coherence stitching everything together, and

Son, touching our hearts, and feeling the ache and exhaustion of the Father's Son, the God-made-man, the gaunt, dusty, tireless fellow who walked and talked endlessly through the hills of Judea, who knew what would happen to him, who accepted it with amazing grace, who died crying out that we might live past death, and

Holy, touching the left shoulder, on which we carry hope, and

Spirit, touching the right shoulder, on which we carry love.

And the gesture is done, hanging in the air like a memory, its line traced on my body as if printed there by the thousands of times my hand has marked it.

Simple, powerful, poignant, the Sign of the Cross is a mnemonic device like the Mass, in which we sit down to table with each other and remember the Last Supper, or a baptism, where we remember John the Baptist's brawny arm pouring some of the Jordan River over Christ. So we remember the central miracle and paradox of the faith that binds us each to each: that we believe, against all evidence and sense, in life and love and light, in the victory of those things over death and evil and darkness. Such a ferocious and brave notion, to be hinted at by such a simple motion, and the gesture itself lasting perhaps all of four seconds.

Simple as the Sign of the Cross is, it carries a brave weight: it names the Trinity, celebrates the Creator, and brings home all the power of faith to the brush of fingers on skin and bone. So do we, sometimes well and sometimes ill, labor to bring home our belief in God's love to the stuff of our daily lives, the skin and bone of this world—and the Sign of the Cross helps us to remember that we have a Companion on the road.

Brian Doyle, '78

PRAYERS FOR MEALS AND FAMILY EXPERIENCES

✠

✠

So whether you eat or drink, or whatever you do,
do everything for the glory of God.
—1 Corinthians 10:31

Our first prayers are learned not in church, but in the home. The family—whatever shape it may take—is, as the *Catechism of the Catholic Church* says, the "domestic church," where children learn to pray. Before meals and before bedtime, we teach children to thank God for blessings bestowed and to ask for God's presence during the good times and bad. There are so many special—and ordinary—times during everyday family life when adults can model prayerfulness for their children. But sometimes they are the ones teaching us.

Traditional Prayers before Meals

Bless us, O Lord,
and these thy gifts,
which we are about to receive
from thy bounty.
Through Christ our Lord.

* * *

Thank you for the food we eat,
Thank you for the world so sweet,
Thank you for the birds that sing,
Thank you God for everything.

* * *

God is great, God is good.
Let us thank him for our food.
By his hands, we are fed.
Let us thank him for our bread.

* * *

Come, Lord Jesus, be our guest,
Let this food to us be blessed.

Children's Grace

Dear God,
I gratefully bow my head
to thank you for my daily bread,
And may there be a goodly share
on every table everywhere.
Simple Prayers of Love and Delight

Irish Grace

May this food restore our strength,
giving new energy to tired limbs,
new thoughts to weary minds.

May this drink restore our souls,
giving vision to dry spirits,
new warmth to cold hearts.

And once refreshed,
may we give new pleasure to you,
who gives us all.
> ***Graces with a Celtic Flavor***

> *The most important thing a father*
> *can do for his children is to love their mother.*
> **Theodore M. Hesburgh, C.S.C.**
> President Emeritus of the University of Notre Dame

Latin American Grace

O God, to those who have hunger give bread,
to those who have bread give the hunger for justice.

Bread Blessing

Lord Jesus Christ, you live and are king forever.
Bread of angels, Bread of everlasting life,
be so kind as to bless this bread
as you blessed the five loaves in the desert,

that all who taste of it may through it
receive health of body and soul.
Roman Ritual

Remembering the Hungry

For food in a world where many walk in hunger;
for faith in a world where many walk in fear;
for friends in a world where many walk alone;
we give you thanks, O Lord.
Huron Hunger Fund

*The family is the "domestic church" where
God's children learn to pray "as the church"
and to persevere in prayer.*
Catechism of the Catholic Church

Grace after Meals

We give you thanks, almighty God,
for these and all your blessings;
you live and reign for ever and ever.

Birthday Blessing for an Adult

Loving God, source of all life,
we give you thanks for the gift of life you have given us.
Hear the prayers of [*name*]
who today celebrates the day of his/her birth
and the gift of life that he/she shares
with family and friends.

Surrounded with your loving presence,
may he/she enjoy many more years
   to praise you
and to share your love with others.
Grant us this through Christ our Lord.
      A Prayer Book for Catholic Families

Birthday Blessing for a Child

Loving God,
you have created each of us
and enfold us in your love.
You have called us each by name
and constantly care for us.
Look with favor on your child, [*name*],
who begins another year of life.
Bless him/her with the joy of your love and friendship.
Give him/her the strength of your grace
that he/she may share your love with family and friends
throughout the coming year.
We ask this through Christ our Lord.
      A Prayer Book for Catholic Families

Prayer for Anniversary of Adoption Day

Today we remember with gratitude
the day [*name*] joined our family,
even though it seems like you have been with us forever.

Today we remember with gratitude
those who cared for you before we did,
who kept you safe and healthy and ready for your new family.

Today we remember with gratitude
the agencies and government workers
who assisted us in the long process of becoming a family.

Today we remember with gratitude
your first parents, your birthmother and birthfather,
who gave you the gift of life.

Today we remember with gratitude
the loving God who brought us together
and who continues to bless this family.
Heidi Schlumpf, '88

As our body cannot live without nourishment, so our soul cannot spiritually be kept alive without prayer.
St. Augustine

Prayer for Families

Dear Lord, keep our family in your divine protection.
Increase our compassion for one another;
give us hearts full of mercy and forgiveness.
Let us speak from a place of love when we share our concerns
with our parents, brothers, and sisters.
Never let a day pass by that we fail to say "I love you."
Increase our gratitude for our gifts and talents
and never let jealousy or a diminished self-esteem
cause us to negatively compare ourselves with family members.
Help our family be your presence to the underserved
and grant us your life-sustaining peace.
Kathleen M. Sullivan, '82 MA, '87 PhD

A Prayer for Parents on Challenging Days

All knowing God,
Help me to stop and breathe when a tough moment arises with
    my child.
Bless me with more patience and awareness when I'm being
    impatient.
Remind me that my temporary bad mood and harsh words
    could create a permanent bad memory for my child.
Forgive me when I get it wrong, and help me to do better.
Also, help me to forgive myself.
Give me the knowledge that taking a little time out for myself
    will make me a better parent,
    and that laughter truly is the best medicine.
Most of all, thank you for giving me the wonderful gift of a
    child,
even on those challenging days.
        Paula J. Biedenharn, '89 MA, '94 PhD

Prayer for Parenting a Special-Needs Child

Dear Lord,
My heart is so tender before you.
At times, the challenges can feel so heavy,
the constant care can be emotionally exhausting and lonely.
Help me to see [*name's*] limitations as limitless opportunities
for me to find strength and courage in you.
Help [*name's*] disability to become my ability
to serve you in such a profound way.
Help me to see through your eyes
the incredible blessing
that you have created him/her to be.
        Penny Hanlon
        Notre Dame Alumni Association

⁘

Searching for a Life Partner

Divine Lover,
you created me to love and be loved.
I desire this love intensely and search for it eternally.
Bless my search for this love as I date.
May I always remember that only you
can fulfill my every desire,
and that love is an active decision.

I ask you to be present and central in my relationships.
Keep my focus on growing closer to you
by growing to love another.
May my love for another mirror your love for me.
Guide me away from the temptations of the flesh
and towards purity.
Allow me to trust,
and help me to always remain trustworthy.

Lead me to desire what is best for those I date
over anything I want from them
and from our relationship.
Remind me always that you have a plan for me,
greater than I could ever imagine.
In your name I pray.
John Sengenberger, '04

Prayer for Loved Ones

The winter will lose its cold,
as the snow will be without whiteness,
the night without darkness,
the heavens without stars,
the day without light.

The flower will lose its beauty,
all fountains their water,
the sea its fish,
the tree its birds,
the forest its beasts,
the earth its harvest—
all these things will pass before
anyone breaks the bonds of our love,
and before I cease caring for you in my heart.
May your days be happy in number as flakes of snow,
may your nights be peaceful,
and may you be without troubles.
Matthew of Rievaulx

A Biblical Blessing

The Lord bless you and keep you!
The Lord let his face shine upon you,
and be gracious to you!
The Lord look upon you kindly and give you peace!
Numbers 6:24–26

Parenting Prayer

Gracious God,
you have honored me with the gift and responsibility of children.
At times I feel inadequate to the task—
unprepared to manage the challenges that spring up at every
stage.
I am in awe of my children,
and of you for entrusting them to me,
and I desire to be the best parent I can be to them.

Fill me with patience and wisdom,
and give me delight and wonder at the miracle that is before me.
Help me to always remember that despite my own shortcomings
or the trials that parenting can bring,
my greatest gift is my steadfast love,
and my strongest ally is you.
I ask this for the sake of your love.

Renee Miller

Single Parent's Prayer

Lord, grant me
time enough
to do all the chores,
join in the games,
help with the lessons,
and say the night prayers,
and still have a few moments left over for me.

Lord, grant me
energy enough
to be bread-baker and breadwinner,
knee-patcher and peacemaker,
ball player and bill juggler.

Lord, grant me
hands enough
to wipe away the tears,
to reach out when I'm needed,
to hug and to hold,
to tickle and touch.

Lord, grant me
heart enough

to share and to care,
to listen and to understand,
and to make a loving home for my family.

Home Blessing

At the entrance:
O God, protect our going out and our coming in;
Let us share the hospitality of this home
with all who visit us,
that those who enter here may know your love and peace.

In the living room:
O God, give your blessings to all who share this room,
that we may be knit together in companionship.

In the kitchen:
O God, you fill the hungry with good things.
Send your blessing on us, as we work in this kitchen,
and make us ever thankful for our daily bread.

In the dining room:
Blessed are you, Lord of heaven and earth,
for you give us food and drink to sustain our lives
and make our hearts glad.
Help us to be grateful for all your mercies,
and mindful of the needs of others.

In the bedrooms:
Protect us, Lord, as we stay awake;
watch over us as we sleep,
that awake we may keep watch with Christ,
and asleep, we may rest in his peace.

In the bathroom:
Blessed are you, Lord of heaven and earth.
You formed us in wisdom and love.
Refresh us in body and in spirit,
and keep us in good health that we might serve you.

Be our shelter, Lord, when we are at home,
our companion when we are away,
and our welcome guest when we return.
And at last receive us into the dwelling place
you have prepared for us in your Father's house,
where you live for ever and ever.

Adapted from *Catholic Household Blessings and Prayers*

Blessing of Children

May the Lord keep you
and make you grow in his love,
so that you may live worthy of the calling he has given you,
now and forever.

Book of Blessings

Parents' Prayer for a Hurting Child

Heavenly Father—Abba,
we praise you and glorify your name.
Thank you for the gift of your Spirit,
who strengthens us in this time of sorrow and pain.
Thank you for your son, Jesus,
who suffered even greater pain for us.
We ask you to protect our child.
Guide [*name*] while he/she is imprisoned

physically, psychologically, or emotionally.
Let [*name*] experience your love and your healing grace
so he/she can believe in his/her lovability and goodness.
Help [*name*] accept your son, Jesus, into his/her life.
We know you hear our prayers, Father,
for you have answered us previously in so many ways!
We ask you this in your Son's name.
> **Kathy and Kevin Misiewicz**
> **Mendoza College of Business**

The family that prays together stays together.
Patrick Peyton, C.S.C.

Chinese Prayer for Parents

When I behold the sacred *liao wo** my thoughts return
to those who begot me, raised me, and now are tired.
I would repay the bounty they have given me,
but it is as the sky: it can never be approached.

*a species of grass symbolizing parenthood

Prayer on a Wedding Anniversary

Lord, you worked your first sign,
a joyful one of abundant and good wine,
at a wedding feast,
to show how you delight in married life.

We thank you for the gift of this vocation,
this sacrament, this life together.
May the years be multiplied,
and their joys ever more so.

✛

May this marital love be a true witness
to your love for us, your Church.
May the graces of this marriage help us to attain
the eternal nuptial feast in your Kingdom.

We praise and thank you,
with your Father and Holy Spirit,
this day and always.
    The Abbey Prayer Book

Prayer for Mother's Day

I offer a prayer for Mother's Day today.
This is who it is for:

It is for all the mothers in this room, in this city,
across this continent, and in every land around this planet.

It is for the mothers whose homes resound with children's
    laughter,
screeching toys, loud music, or the sullen teenage shrug.
It is for the mothers who gave birth in joy or in agony or in grief.

It is for the mothers who have adopted the motherless
and discovered how wide love can reach;
and it is for the mothers who have given over their children to
    others.
This prayer is for all the women who have wished to be mothers
    and are not.

It is for all the mothers whose children have ever gone off to war,
for the worry they endure and the tension they carry through
    every hour of absence.

It is for the mothers whose children return whole and unscathed,
or who return wounded in mind or body, or who do not return
   at all.

It is for all the mothers who grieve—
lost pregnancies, lost children, lost hopes, lost futures.

And this is my prayer:
May peace come to you.
Peace amid the noise and chaos of active children
Peace amid the silence and the absence.
Peace with the choices you have made,
the paths taken and the ones not taken.
Peace with the grief you have endured.
May peace come to you,
and may you greet it and welcome it,
and make a place for it to live within you.
May peace find a home in you,
and from that home, may peace venture widely over this earth.
   Jill Ann Terwilliger

Prayer for Father's Day

Let us praise those fathers who have striven to balance the
demands of work, marriage, and children with an honest
awareness of both joy and sacrifice.

Let us praise those fathers who, lacking a good model for a
father, have worked to become a good father.

Let us praise those fathers who by their own account were not
always there for their children, but who continue to offer those
children, now grown, their love and support.

Let us pray for those fathers who have been wounded by the neglect and hostility of their children.

Let us praise those fathers who, despite divorce, have remained in their children's lives.

Let us praise those fathers whose children are adopted, and whose love and support has offered healing.

Let us praise those fathers who, as stepfathers, freely chose the obligation of fatherhood and earned their stepchildren's love and respect.

Let us praise those fathers who have lost a child to death, and continue to hold the child in their heart.

Let us praise those men who have no children, but cherish the next generation as if they were their own.

Let us praise those men who have "fathered" us in their role as mentors and guides.

Let us praise those men who are about to become fathers; may they openly delight in their children.

And let us praise those fathers who have died, but live on in our memory and whose love continues to nurture us.

Kirk Loadman-Copeland

Prayer for Military Families

Almighty Father, watch over my family,
encourage them when we are separated during deployments,
and give them health of mind and body
that they may serve you with perfect love
until the day when we,
with all who have served you,
will rejoice in your presence for ever.
> ***Armed with the Faith***

Prayer for Grandparents Raising a Grandchild

Dear God,
We thank you for the gift and the challenge to parent our
grandchild.
We do not understand every experience in our lives
nor the full extent of your divine purpose.
What we do know, however, is your promise to remain always
faithful to us.
We pray for your continued guidance, patience, and strength
to do what you have called us to do.
And we pray that our efforts
in parenting this young life will be fruitful.
> **Janet and Pete Miller**
> **Notre Dame Alumni Association**

Prayer for Family Reunion

We bless your name, O Lord,
for sending your own incarnate Son,
to become part of a family,
so that, as he lived his life,
he would experience its worries and its joys.

We ask you, Lord,
to protect and watch over this family,
so that in the strength of your grace
its members may enjoy prosperity,
possess the priceless gift of your peace,
and, as the church alive in the home,
bear witness in this world to your glory.
Catholic Household Blessings and Prayers

4

GLORY AND PRAISE TO OUR GOD

Prayers of Praise and Celebration

✤ THE LOG CHAPEL ✤

When I think of the Log Chapel, I think of similar places around the world where I have been. One is the meditation room at the United Nations. Dag Hammarskjöld called it "a room of quiet where only thoughts should speak." I remember especially the opening sentence of the brochure he wrote for the room: "We all have within us a center of stillness surrounded by silence."

I think also of the Church of the Poor Devil (*Igreja do Pobre Diablo*) that I found on the Amazon River. I wrote a book with that title about the religion of the poor. It too was a little wedding chapel like our Log Chapel where I have celebrated weddings and baptisms.

A third such place is the Chapel of Notre Dame du Haut at Ronchamp in France, designed by Le Corbusier. I have never been there, and have only seen photos of it and read Le Corbusier's brochure on it. In setting out his vision for the place he was to design, he stressed that it must be a labor of love, it must express a relationship with God, and it must be on a human scale. Much of what he said of Ronchamp is true as well of the Log Chapel. The essential thing is the relationship with God.

I think too of a hut I saw along the Amazon with a sign over the door, *Fe em Deus,* Faith in God.

John Dunne, C.S.C.
Department of Theology

✤ LORD OF THE DANCE ✤

I hear the grumblings about liturgical dance, but I ignore them. At the opening Mass each year, at the Mass on the day of my inauguration as president of Saint Mary's, and at every "special" Saint Mary's Mass for which they are available, I ask our liturgical dancers to lead us in their special kind of prayer, the kind of prayer that moves their entire bodies in praise of God.

The criticisms of liturgical dance run the gamut from "it's not good dance" (but, actually, sometimes it is very good), to "it is distracting" (but, then should we not do away with the distraction of music, stained glass, murals, etc.?), to "it just does not belong in church." Certainly, if we are to incorporate dance into our communal prayer life, the dance should be as technically good as we can muster. So, too, with singing. But, in my opinion, neither art form should be banished from our liturgies just because better execution can be found elsewhere.

Liturgical dance came into my life through our four daughters, all of whom danced enthusiastically and joyfully to the "Lord of the Dance" on numerous Pentecost Sundays at our parish family Mass. No such thing ever took place in my childhood. Seeing the joy our children took in this type of prayer cracked open the door of my awareness to forms of prayers other than those said on one's knees in a pew or at the side of the bed.

One Holy Saturday Vigil Mass, our oldest daughter danced a solo as part of the celebration. She was eleven or twelve, and I distinctly remember the flowing, flowery knit dress she wore as she bowed and twirled before the altar of the Lord. I was enthralled. At the conclusion of the Mass, our pastor called her forward to thank her and to have her curtsey to the assembled congregation. I could barely see her because my eyes were filled with tears. Of course, motherly pride was part of what I was feeling. But what really moved me was that our child had, as she would have said, "put herself out there." All alone and with her whole being she danced a dance of joy. Why? For the beauty of the liturgy. For the assembled faithful. For God. What more could a mother ask than to see her daughter literally bow to God?

As Catholics we do not divide the sacred from the physical realities. Instead we understand the miracle of the Incarnation as having blessed those realities. Indeed, our strong tradition of religious art—painting, sculpture, music, architecture, and dance—is a manifestation of our belief in the sacramentality of the physical as well as a recognition of our human need to engage not just our mind but also our senses in our attempts to understand and worship God.

I have never done liturgical dance, nor do I believe anyone would want me to do so. But I have sensed the powerful prayer that body movement can be. Before students return to the Saint Mary's campus each fall, the faculty, administrators, and staff of the college gather for a forum, which begins with a prayer led by the college president. Every time I stand before the assembled community and extend my arms to lead the prayer, I am struck by the power and vulnerability of the *orans* posture. It is a good posture for praying to God, but a scary one to assume in front of a large group of people. It is also a posture of love and inclusion; it is a posture from which one can embrace the many. The extension of my arms in a gesture that I have seen repeated hundreds and perhaps thousands of times in my life is itself a prayer, its own dance of love of God and of the assembly.

I am a lawyer, and words are my métier. But my most fervent prayers come from somewhere within me that is not verbal, and the formulation of those prayers into words sometimes strikes me as a process of reduction. Words—except those of a truly talented poet or a wonderful comedian—seldom grip me to my core. So why should we limit prayer to something we "say"?

Carol Ann Mooney, '77
President, Saint Mary's College

PRAYERS OF PRAISE AND CELEBRATION

✢✢

O Lord, open my lips,
and my mouth will declare your praise.
—Psalm 51:15

Y ou got the job. She said yes to your proposal. The tests came back negative. Some days you feel like walking down the street screaming, "God is good." The challenge, of course, is to remember to praise God when life is humming along normally. The liturgy includes prayers of praise, and the writings of many saints throughout history feature words praising God's goodness. So even when you're not on a high, remember to praise God. As they say in African American churches, "God is good, all the time. All the time, God is good."

Te Deum

You are God: we praise you;
you are the Lord: we acclaim you;
you are the eternal Father: all creation worships you.

To you all angels, all the powers of heaven,
Cherubim and Seraphim, sing in endless praise:
    Holy, holy, holy Lord, God of power and might,
    heaven and earth are full of your glory.

The glorious company of apostles praise you.
The noble fellowship of prophets praise you.
The white-robed army of martyrs praise you.

Throughout the world the holy Church acclaims you;
    Father, of majesty unbounded,
    your true and only Son, worthy of all worship,
    and the Holy Spirit, advocate and guide.

You, Christ, are the king of glory,
the eternal Son of the Father.

When you became man to set us free
you did not shun the Virgin's womb.

You overcame the sting of death,
and opened the kingdom of heaven to all believers.

You are seated at God's right hand in glory.
We believe that you will come, and be our judge.

Come then, Lord, and help your people,
bought with the price of your own blood,
and bring us with your saints
to glory everlasting.

Joy Comes with the Morning

Sing praises to the Lord,
O you his faithful ones,
and give thanks to his holy name.
For his anger is but for a moment;
his favor is for a lifetime.
Weeping may linger for the night,
but joy comes with the morning.
Psalm 30:4–5

Son, in thirty-five years of religious study,
I have only come up with two hard,
incontrovertible facts: there is a God, and . . .
I am not him.
John Cavanaugh, C.S.C., in *Rudy*

Prayer of Praise

O Lord in whom all things live,
who commanded us to seek you,
who are always ready to be found:
to know you is life,
to serve you is freedom,
to praise you is our soul's delight.
We bless you and adore you,
we worship you and magnify you,
we give thanks to you for your great glory,
through Jesus Christ our Lord.
St. Augustine

Blessed Are You, God of Life

Blessed are you, God of life,
Maker of heaven and earth.

You scatter the stars in the darkness.
You fire the sun to brighten the day
and the moon to reflect your light.

In the depths of the earth and the oceans
you sow the seeds of life.
From beginnings we cannot see,
you draw forth a web of life:
algae and bacteria, green plants and trees,
insects and lizards, birds and mammals,
creatures both strange and wonderful.

By your Wisdom you call forth humankind,
female and male, in your image made,
of every color, culture, and tongue.
In them your Spirit draws forth freedom
to love and to serve and to sing your praise.

All your works give thanks:
How marvelous the work of your hands!
With one voice we cry out in joy:
blessed are you, God of life,
Maker of heaven and earth,
unto endless ages, now and forever.
     David Lysik, '90

Beautiful

God, make us beautiful:
radiant and dazzling,
your holy light shining through us,
appealing and lavish,
a sign of your abundant love,
striking and attractive,
your divine providence realized in the here and now,
pristine, free of blemish or stain,
healed and made new through your mercy.
Let all know that beauty is not skin deep,
but comes from the core of us,
hearts afire with your Sacred Spirit.
May all we do and all we are make known what beauty truly is,
to be filled with God's blessings.
Paul Michael Ybarra, C.S.C.

An African Canticle

All you big things, bless the Lord:
Mount Kilimanjaro and Lake Victoria,
the Rift Valley and the Serengeti Plain,
fat baobabs and shady mango trees,
all eucalyptus and tamarind trees,
bless the Lord.
Praise and extol him for ever and ever.

All you tiny things, bless the Lord:
busy black ants and hopping fleas,
wriggling tadpoles and mosquito larvae,
flying locusts and water drops,
pollen dust and tsetse flies,

millet seed and dried *dagaa*,
bless the Lord.
Praise and extol him for ever and ever.
Traditional African Prayer

The fullness of joy is to behold God in everything.
St. Julian of Norwich

Canticle of Brother Sun and Sister Moon

Most high, all powerful, all good Lord!
All praise is yours, all glory, all honor, and all blessing.
To you, alone, Most High, do they belong.
No mortal lips are worthy to pronounce your name.

Be praised, my Lord, through all your creatures,
especially through my lord Brother Sun,
who brings the day; and you give light through him.
And he is beautiful and radiant in all his splendor!
Of you, Most High, he bears the likeness.

Be praised, my Lord, through Sister Moon and the stars;
in the heavens you have made them bright, precious and
    beautiful.

Be praised, my Lord, through Brothers Wind and Air,
and clouds and storms, and all the weather,
through which you give your creatures sustenance.

Be praised, My Lord, through Sister Water;
she is very useful, and humble, and precious, and pure.

Be praised, my Lord, through Brother Fire,
through whom you brighten the night.
He is beautiful and cheerful, and powerful and strong.

Be praised, my Lord, through our sister Mother Earth,
who feeds us and rules us,
and produces various fruits with colored flowers and herbs.

Be praised, my Lord, through those who forgive for love of you;
through those who endure sickness and trial.

Happy those who endure in peace,
for by you, Most High, they will be crowned.

Be praised, my Lord, through our Sister Bodily Death,
from whose embrace no living person can escape.
Woe to those who die in mortal sin!
Happy those she finds doing your most holy will.
The second death can do no harm to them.

Praise and bless my Lord, and give thanks,
and serve him with great humility.
   St. Francis of Assisi

May You Be Blessed Forever

May you be blessed forever, Lord,
for not abandoning me when I abandoned you.
May you be blessed forever, Lord,
for offering your hand of love in my darkest, most lonely
  moment.
May you be blessed forever, Lord,
for putting up with such a stubborn soul as mine.
May you be blessed forever, Lord,
for loving me more than I love myself.

May you be blessed forever, Lord,
for continuing to pour out your blessings upon me,
even though I respond so poorly.
May you be blessed forever, Lord,
for drawing out the goodness in all people,
even including me.
May you be blessed forever, Lord,
for repaying our sin with your love.
May you be blessed forever, Lord,
for being constant and unchanging,
amidst all the changes of the world.
May you be blessed forever, Lord,
for your countless blessings on me and on all your creatures.
St. Teresa of Avila

Praise to the Trinity

To the Trinity be praise!
God is music, God is life
that nurtures every creature in its kind.
Our God is the song of the angel throng
and the splendor of secret ways
hid from all humankind,
But God our life is the life of all.
Hildegard of Bingen

Blessing and Glory to God

Salvation belongs to our God
who is seated on the throne, and to the Lamb!
Amen! Blessing and glory and wisdom
and thanksgiving and honor

⊹

and power and might
be to our God for ever and ever!
Revelation 7:10, 12

The Divine Praises

Blessed be God.
Blessed be his Holy Name.
Blessed be Jesus Christ, true God and true man.
Blessed be the name of Jesus.
Blessed be his most Sacred Heart.
Blessed be Jesus in the most holy sacrament of the altar.
Blessed be the Holy Spirit, the Paraclete.
Blessed be the great Mother of God, Mary most holy.
Blessed be her holy and Immaculate Conception.
Blessed be her glorious Assumption.
Blessed be the name of Mary, Virgin and Mother.
Blessed be Saint Joseph, her most chaste spouse.
Blessed be God in his angels and in his saints.

Make a Joyful Noise

Make a joyful noise to the Lord, all the earth.
Worship the Lord with gladness;
come into his presence with singing.

Know that the Lord is God.
It is he that made us, and we are his;
we are his people, and the sheep of his pasture.

Enter his gates with thanksgiving,
and his courts with praise.
Give thanks to him, bless his name.

For the Lord is good;
his steadfast love endures forever,
and his faithfulness to all generations.
Psalm 100

Rejoice in the Way Things Are

Be content with what you have;
rejoice in the way things are.
When you realize there is nothing lacking
the whole world belongs to you.
Lao-Tzu

*Don't pray when it rains if you don't
pray when the sun shines.*
Satchel Paige

In Celebration of God's Goodness

You are holy, Lord, the only God,
and your deeds are wonderful.
You are strong.
You are great.
You are the Most High.
You are Almighty.
You, Holy Father, are King of heaven and earth.
You are Three and One, Lord God, all Good.
You are Good, all Good, supreme Good,
Lord God, living and true.
You are love. You are wisdom.
You are humility. You are endurance.

You are rest. You are peace.
You are joy and gladness.
You are justice and moderation.
You are all our riches, and you suffice for us.
You are beauty.
You are gentleness.
You are our protector.
You are our guardian and defender.
You are our courage.
You are our haven and our hope.
You are our faith, our great consolation.
You are our eternal life, Great and Wonderful Lord,
God Almighty, Merciful Savior.
St. Francis of Assisi

Final Doxology

Praise the Lord! Praise God in his sanctuary;
praise him in his mighty firmament!
Praise him for his mighty deeds;
praise him according to his surpassing greatness!

Praise him with trumpet sound;
praise him with lute and harp!
Praise him with tambourine and dance;
praise him with strings and pipe!
Praise him with clanging cymbals;
praise him with loud clashing cymbals!
Let everything that breathes praise the Lord!
Praise the Lord!
Psalm 150

5

WORK OF HUMAN HANDS

Prayers for Work and Study

THE HESBURGH
LIBRARY

In the beginning was the Word. . . .

"You are in a nomad zone," the sign says when I walk into the reference section of the library this afternoon. Fair enough, I think; I'll be a mental roamer, grazing among truths and ideas, seeking sustenance in distant pastures, climbing vicarious peaks. Though an inspection of smaller print on the sign reveals the "zone" to be a wireless network, I like my first impression better: I am a nomad wandering in a research library, a great repository of words. And "Word" is the very symbol that St. John used for the second person of God.

All words are symbols—sounds strung together to stand for a fruit, or a particular child, or an ache in the heart. Words allow us to transfer what we think or know to someone else, to open ourselves to be known by that other. So it's not surprising that St. John used "Word" as a symbol for Jesus, who opened himself that we might know more of God. The written word—which uses symbols for the sounds of language—allows us to transport those words over distance or down through time. If I believe—and I do—in an incarnate world, then the words contained in this tower of words—this poem by Yeats, this scientific theory, this history of the Ottoman Empire—may help me, just as the one Word did, to know the unknowable God.

Sonia Gernes
Professor Emeritus of English

LORD, TEACH
✛ US TO PRAY ✛

Jesus taught his disciples to pray. Can we do the same? Can prayer be taught?

Of course, theology students learn about prayer in a number of their courses, but a special course at Notre Dame has tried to teach college students how to pray. Called simply, "Catholic Prayer," it is one of a series of optional, one-credit "Know Your Catholic Faith" classes taught by the theology department. These courses are by design both academic and experiential.

Although not claiming to be a master of the spiritual life in general or the life of prayer in particular, I have taught the class about ten times over the last seven years. My task, as a theologian, is simply to give these students some entry into the rich life of prayer as it has developed and grown in the living tradition of the Church. Inspired by the final (and, by miles, the best) part of the *Catechism of the Catholic Church*, the weeks we spend together are an opportunity for me to open up to them the accumulated wealth of the Catholic tradition of prayer.

We typically meet on five or six consecutive Sunday evenings for a little over an hour of classroom lecture and discussion after which, as a class, we walk over to the Basilica of the Sacred Heart on campus to participate in Sunday Vespers. On the first evening some introductory notions about the Church's liturgical prayer in general and vespers in particular are discussed.

We try to survey both liturgical prayer and a fair representative sample of devotional practices as well as some introduction to the practice of meditation and contemplative prayer.

For texts I have used everything from a little catechism on the psalms in question-and-answer format (written by myself) to Michael Casey's very useful book on prayer in the Western tradition called *Towards God*. I am quite keen on Casey's book because it is so well written, so theologically rich, and so practical in its pastoral observations. One basic principle I teach is that the act of prayer—whether personal or liturgical—is, by its very nature as a decision to pray, also an act of faith. The decision to pray involves a fundamental conversion (a turning) toward God and, in the same moment, an aversion from that which is not focused on God. The corollary of that principle is that all prayer, no matter how distracted or rote, is good prayer.

The other foundational idea taught in this course is that being a person of prayer does not demand elaborate strategies or reams of books or the searching out of location. Borrowing a phrase from the patristic tradition, to be a person of prayer is to be one who in daily life "remembers God." The practical consequence of this truth is that we should pay attention to those simple acts by which we can easily remember God: by a simple act of prayer at rising, at meals, in the evening, and in those moments (when we study, work out, etc.) that punctuate our days. It is useful to recall that the Italian verb "to remember" is *ricordare*, which means, literally, "to call back to the heart."

And the students who take this Catholic prayer course? Some come with hesitations, doubts, or problems relative to their spiritual life, while others come to enrich themselves and deepen their prayer lives. Their reflections vary, with some predictable enough and others startling in the depths of their own prayer experiences. I never require them to be autobiographical in their final brief reflection essay, but many of them are.

Those of us who teach the "Know Your Catholic Faith" courses do so as volunteers. But I know that my effort is amply rewarded just to know that many of the students who graduate will do so with far more than a book knowledge of their Christian faith.

Lawrence S. Cunningham
Department of Theology

PRAYERS FOR WORK AND STUDY

Whatever you do, work at it with all your heart,
as working for the Lord, not for men.
—Colossians 3:23

So many of our waking hours are spent in work or study, but too often we fail to think of these endeavors as opportunities for prayer—except when we fear we may lose our job or face a particularly challenging exam. Perhaps modern-day workers and students can learn from monastics who stressed the importance of an integrated life of work and prayer. Whether preparing for a profession, looking for work, struggling with people at work, or trying to balance work with the rest of life, we can turn to God for help and a listening ear.

Lord of All Hopefulness

Lord of all hopefulness, Lord of all joy,
whose trust ever childlike, no cares can destroy,

be there at our waking, and give us, we pray,
your bliss in our hearts, Lord, at the break of the day.

Lord of all eagerness, Lord of all faith,
whose strong hands were skilled at the plane and the lathe,
be there at our labors, and give us, we pray,
your strength in our hearts, Lord, at the noon of the day.

Lord, of all kindliness, Lord of all grace,
your hands swift to welcome, your arms to embrace,
be there at our homing, and give us, we pray,
your love in our hearts, Lord, at the eve of the day.

Lord of all gentleness, Lord of all calm,
whose voice is contentment, whose presence is balm,
be there at our sleeping, and give us, we pray,
your peace in our hearts, Lord, at the end of the day.
Jan Struther

Prayer to St. Joseph the Worker

Glorious St. Joseph,
model of all those who are devoted to labor,
obtain for me the grace to work conscientiously,
putting the call of duty above my many sins;
to work with thankfulness and joy,
considering it an honor to employ and develop,
by means of labor, the gifts received from God;
to work with order, peace, prudence, and patience,
never surrendering to weariness or difficulties;
to work, above all, with purity of intention,
and with detachment from self,
having always death before my eyes
and the account which I must render of time lost,

of talents wasted, of good omitted,
of vain complacency in success so fatal to the work of God.
All for Jesus, all for Mary,
all after thy example, O Patriarch Joseph.
Such shall be my motto in life and death.

Prayer for Discernment of a Vocation

Lord,
what is the life you are calling me to live?
Who is it that you are calling me to be?
There seems to be so many answers, yet I know
that you have laid out a path for me.
Send your Spirit to guide me as I discern your path.
Help me listen to your voice in the stillness of my heart
amid the many distractions and temptations of life.
Help me understand and see
the gifts and talents you have given me,
not as the world sees them but as you do.
Give me the strength to listen to you intently,
and to follow your path courageously.
Brian Ching, C.S.C.

Boss's Prayer

Christ our Lord,
you refused the way of domination
and died the death of a slave.
May we also refuse to lord it
over those who are subject to us,

but share the weight of authority
so that all may be empowered
in your name.
Janet Morley

For Conflict with a Coworker or Friend

Lord,
I heard your voice today.
You said something I'd rather not hear.
I prayed about that awkward person, you know,
the one that drives me mad.
I reminded you how often
I've been hurt, annoyed, irritated, and upset.
And you said, "Love one another as I have loved you."
Pam Weaver

Prayer for Meetings

Almighty God, Ruler of the Universe,
by your power we move and have our being.
We are gathered here today to serve you
and conduct the affairs of [*name the facility*].
Give us knowledge and strength to do your will,
with a proper balance of eternal values and our present needs.
May we accept our responsibilities and act with courage,
considering the feelings of other people.
Grant us a sense of justice and stewardship
both now and forever.
Benedictine Health System

Prayer for Labor Day

God give me work till my life shall end
and life till my work is done.
Epitaph of Winifred Holtby, British Author

*Our life is work. [Father Sorin's] own life was
all work—wondrous work!—and it is God's
will that every event in our lives, sorrowful
or joyous, should be an occasion to animate
ourselves to the accomplishment of the work
that lies before us.*

From a sermon at Father Edward Sorin's funeral

May There Always Be Work

May there always be work for your hands to do.
May your purse always hold a coin or two.
May the sun always shine upon your window pane.
May a rainbow be certain to follow each rain.
May the hand of a friend always be near to you and
may God fill your heart with gladness to cheer you.
Traditional Irish Blessing

Prayer for Discernment I

Almighty God,
in whom we live and move and have our being,
you have made us for yourself,
and our hearts are restless until they find their rest in you.
Grant us purity of heart and strength of purpose,

that no selfish passion may hinder us from knowing your will;
no weakness from doing it;
but that in your light we may see light
and in your service we may find perfect freedom.
      St. Augustine

Prayer for Discernment II

Teach us, good Lord, to serve you as you deserve;
to give and not to count the cost;
to fight and not to heed the wounds;
to toil and not to seek for rest;
to labor and not to ask for any reward,
save that of knowing we do your will.
      St. Ignatius of Loyola

Prayer for a Difficult Work Environment

Lord, as I enter this workplace,
I bring your presence with me.
I ask that you bring your peace, your grace, your mercy
and your perfect order into this office.
I acknowledge your power over all that will be
spoken, thought, decided, and done within these walls.
I commit to using my gifts responsibly in your honor.
Lord, when I am confused, guide me.
When I am weary, energize me.
When I am burned out, infuse me
with the light of the Holy Spirit.

Prayer to Find Employment

Dear St. Joseph,
you were yourself once faced with the responsibility
of providing the necessities of life for Jesus and Mary.
Look down with fatherly compassion upon me
in my anxiety over my present inability to support my family.
Please help me to find gainful employment very soon,
so that this heavy burden of concern will be lifted from my heart
and so that I am soon able to provide
for those whom God has entrusted to my care.
Help me to guard against bitterness and discouragement,
so that I may emerge from this trial spiritually enriched
and with even greater blessings from God.

At Work within My Nature

Give success to the work of my hands, O Lord,
especially when my mind is at play,
for there I so easily rationalize, stress, and confound
the movement of your grace
which through my hands
fulfills a mission greater than any task
to which I might put them,
lest it be the vanity of vanities
to which I lend a hand
and fail to touch upon the depth and breadth
of the infinite and compassionate love
in which you hold me—spirit, mind, and body.
Kevin Sandberg, C.S.C.

Prayer for Teachers

Jesus, you taught with words and by example—
    but always out of love.
Please guide me during this school day
to create a positive learning environment for my students.
Give me strength to meet the needs of my diverse learners.
Give me patience when moments are trying.
Give me creativity to develop engaging lessons.
Give me humility to recognize
    when my students are teaching me.
And give me a loving heart
so that I may always teach out of love, just as you did.
        Meredith McCarthy, '95

*The mind will not be cultivated at the
expense of the heart.*
Blessed Basile Moreau, C.S.C.
Founder of the Congregation of Holy Cross

Prayer for Lawyers

God of all justice, mercy, and love;
thank you for the gifts which enable us to serve as attorneys;
give us the understanding, courage, wisdom, and prudence
so that we might use your gifts to assist in creating
a just societal order that respects individual dignity
and advances the common good.

Enlighten our minds with a concern
for the poor, oppressed, and powerless,
and inflame our wills so that we might
act to lift their burdens.

With St. Thomas More as our patron,
grant us the grace to live and work humbly
with eternal salvation always before our eyes.

John J. Coughlin, O.F.M.
The Law School

Prayer for Engineers

Merciful and loving Father, We humbly come before you
recognizing that all good things come from you. We thank you
for the bountiful blessings that you have bestowed on us: our
lives, our talents and abilities, and our recognition that we come
from you and are destined to return to you.

We pray for the success of our work, the work of engineers done
in service of society. Inspire us, O Lord, as we analyze, critique,
design, create, and prudentially judge works in service of your
sons and daughters. Give us knowledge, wisdom, understanding,
prudence, care, and fortitude to perform our work, and, if it be
your will, bless our work and make it fruitful.

Make our work beneficial and effective to bless your children, to
decrease suffering, and to improve the quality of life throughout
the world for all of our brothers and sisters in Christ.

We pray that we will always have your heart of compassion and
love as we strive to serve those in need. May our work be an
extension of your work in the world.

We ask also for the intercession of your servant, St. Joseph, the
spouse of Our Mother Notre Dame, and the patron saint of
engineering.

Peter Kilpatrick
College of Engineering

Prayer for Scientists

God give me unclouded eyes and freedom from haste.
God give me quiet and relentless anger against all pretense
and all pretentious work and all work left slack and unfinished.
God give me a restlessness whereby I may neither sleep nor
    accept praise
till my observed results equal my calculated results
or in pious glee I discover and assault my error.
      Sinclair Lewis

Prayer for Healthcare Workers

Heavenly Father, center of our lives, we ask for your blessing as
we begin our day ministering to your children and each other.
May we see your face in all persons who enter our lives today,
and be an instrument of your perfect love.

Heavenly Father, healer of all, be with us as we do your work
with the skills you have blessed us with. May we provide
acceptance, reassurance, and comfort to a patient who may be
frightened or facing an illness or injury alone for the first time in
their life.

Heavenly Father, creator of all, keep us from being judgmental
of a patient who needs our comfort and care when their
behavior has caused illness or harm. Let us tend to them with
unconditional acceptance, and offer guidance with compassion
to help mend their broken body and spirit.

Heavenly Father, center of all hope, provide wisdom in our
words that offer empathy and support to angry, grieving, or
denying parents, as they learn their child is facing an illness they

are not prepared for. May we ease their fears with open and honest dialogue.

Heavenly Father, renewer of spirit, give us patience when the days are long and we are weary. Provide us the strength we need to work those extra hours when your children need our care and relief cannot be found. Keep our minds illuminated with your light, so we will not falter in your work.

Heavenly Father, receiver of prayer, when this day ends, may we praise you in thanksgiving for the gift of life and the special blessings you have provided us as vessels of your healing power. May your peace be with us as we await the restorative power of sleep.

Ann E. Kleva
University Health Services

Prayer for Counselors

Dear God,
help those who come for help
to know they are loved by you
unconditionally.
Relieve them of unnecessary anxieties.
Bestow your gift of hope lavishly upon them.
Heal their emotional hurts.
Infuse in them forgiveness.
And please do all the same
for those of us who call ourselves
helpers.

Susan Steibe-Pasalich
University Counseling Center

✣

Prayer for Police Officers

Good and just God, our Father,
bestow on us, your servants in law enforcement;
ears to hear the truth and tongues to speak it;
strong hands to do justice with grace and compassion;
arms to protect those who need protection;
courage and legs to stand when others fall;
the Spirit and will to serve all those you love,
no matter how unlovely;
character that is beyond reproach;
and hearts to love as you love.

May we bind up the brokenhearted,
may we proclaim freedom for the true captives,
may we comfort and provide for all who mourn and grieve,
may we elicit praise rather than despair.

For you are the Lord.
You love justice and hate iniquity.
Forgive us for the times we have failed
to do, think, love, serve, and protect as you do.

Help us rebuild and restore the ruined and devastated.
May we renew the ruined cities
that have been devastated for generations.
Give us your heart for all the people.
In Christ's name we pray.
   Keri Kei Shibata
   Notre Dame Security Police

Prayer for Librarians

Father, you have declared that your Word is living and powerful,
and discerns the thoughts and intents of the heart.
Help me to abide in you, as your Son instructs,
so that my mind may be illuminated by your truth
in carrying out the work which you have given me to do.
Grant that I see the remainder of my natural life
as your workmanship and not my own.
I ask these things in the name of your Son, Jesus Christ,
who redeemed me from my sins
and lives in me through your Holy Spirit.
> **Alan Krieger**
> **Hesburgh Libraries**

Prayer for Actors

Dearest Creator, from whose limitless knowledge, imagination,
and action
spring the myriad variations of humanity,
thank you for our special abilities
to bring the imagined to demonstrable life
in front of all who see and hear;
and thank you for the courage you grant us
to plumb the depths and heights of being human,
and the healing your belief in us brings to our necessary
vulnerability.

Grant actors compassionate love
for all the individual creatures you devise,
so that we may use our gifts of interpretation to the fullest.

Let us seek to show human truth, so that we may
learn and teach, enjoy, and entertain,
and bring your Light and Love to life on stage.
Denise Blank, '86, '10 MNA

*I've found that prayers work best when you
have big players.*
Knute Rockne

Prayer for Coaches

Lord, lay down your path
between the lines of battle
where many leaders have before me walked.

Lay down your path
so I may tread in the footsteps
of the wise, courageous, and fallen faithful;
for the victorious road has yet to be paved with gold.

Lay down your path
so these spirited athletes know not the prospect
of laying down
but believe in the glory revealed in your way.

When the contest approaches
and this game we love becomes a way of life,
give me the strength to lead with a narrowing focus.

We arrive today as a team prepared
to meet each twisted mile with steps undaunted.
Our sights are set. . . .
Lord, lay down your path.
Dylan Drugan, '06

Prayer for Farmers

O God,
who taught Adam the simple art of tilling the soil,
and who through Jesus Christ, the true vine,
revealed yourself the husbandman of our souls,
deign, we pray, through the merits of blessed Isidore,
to instill into our hearts a horror of sin and a love of prayer,
so that, working the soil in the sweat of our brow,
we may enjoy eternal happiness in heaven,
through the same Christ our Lord.

Prayer for Writers

Blessed are you, O Lord our God. From the very moment you first circumscribed eternity for this mysterious universe that surrounds us, the fascinating geography of earth where we struggle to dwell together in peace, we have been hallowed with signs that all reality is sacred, all is grace by your will and good pleasure.

With each succeeding generation, your people have sought to write words that speak, sometimes well, sometimes poorly, of all that reminds them of the divine wisdom and goodness that is displayed round about for all to see.

Now, Lord God, as I gaze at this screen before me that is yet blank, send your spirit upon this intent of mine, that good plan you have formed in me to bring a small increment of wisdom to those who long for wisdom.

May pride and hubris not detract me from the task of writing simply and unashamedly of my human weakness and of the glory that surrounds me, where evidence of your goodness overwhelms me.

Lord God, author divine, let all who write words and utter sounds strive to follow none other than the pattern you set when our desert ancestors first asked your name and you said: "Write YHWH."

Thus shall we continue to write until our search for true wisdom reveals you to us, face to face. At that moment in eternity, Lord God, there will be no further need to write words.
LeRoy E. Clementich, C.S.C.

Prayer for the Army

Lord God of hosts,
stretch forth, we pray, your almighty arm
to strengthen and protect the soldiers of our country.
Support them in the day of battle;
and in the time of test and training
keep them safe from all evil.
Endow them with courage and loyalty;
and grant that in all things they may serve without reproach.
Armed with the Faith

Prayer for the Navy

Eternal Lord God,
you alone spread the heavens and rule the raging sea.

Take into your most gracious protection
our country's Navy and all who serve therein.
Preserve them from the dangers of the sea
and from the violence of the enemy,
that they may be a safeguard unto the United States of America,
and a security for such as sail upon the seas
in peaceful and lawful missions.
In serving you, O Lord, may our sailors serve their country.
Armed with the Faith

Prayer for the Marine Corps

Eternal Father,
we commend to your protection and care
the members of the Marine Corps.
Guide and direct them in the defense of our country
and in the maintenance of justice among the nations.
Sustain them in the hour of danger.
Grant that wherever they serve
they may be loyal to their high traditions,
and that at all times they may put their trust in you.
Armed with the Faith

Prayer for the Air Force

Lord God of hosts,
you stretch out the heavens like a curtain.
Watch over and protect, we pray, the airmen of our country
as they fly upon their appointed tasks.
Give them courage as they face the foe,
and skill in the performance of their duty.
Sustain them with your everlasting arms.
May your hand lead them,

and your right hand hold them up,
that they may return to the earth
with a grateful sense of your mercy.
Armed with the Faith

*I hope you come to find that which gives life a deep
meaning for you, something worth living for, maybe
even worth dying for, something that energizes you,
enthuses you, enables you to keep moving ahead.*

Ita Ford

Prayer for the Coast Guard

Lord our God,
who stilled the raging seas by your word of power,
watch over, we pray you, the men and women of the Coast
    Guard
as they sail upon their missions of vigilant aid.
Grant them courage and skill and a safe return.
Fill them with a grateful sense of your mercy toward them.
Armed with the Faith

Prayer for Students

Lord Jesus,
you were once a student like me.
You studied God's law,
the history of your people,
and a trade by which to earn a living.
You lived in a human family,
made steady progress in understanding,
and yearned to discover your vocation in life.

Open my mind to the truth of things,
make me humble before the awesome mysteries of the universe,
make me proud to be a human being and a child of God,
and give me courage to live my life in the light of your gospel.
Day by Day

Study Prayer

O Lord, how worthless this knowledge would be,
if it were not for the enlightening of my mind for thy service,
or for making me more useful to my fellow men.
St. Elizabeth Ann Seton

Students' Prayer

God, there is so much to know and discover about our world.
Thank you for the sun, moon, and stars,
the earth and all that is in it!
Thank you for giving me life.
Help me to do my work well.
Inspire me to discover my talents.
Open my heart and mind to new ideas.
When I feel like giving up or not giving my best,
renew my spirit.
I pray that my education helps me
to better serve you, your creation, and all your people.
Through my studies allow me to learn more about myself
that I might grow in grace.
And, Lord, draw me closer to you, day by day.
Katie Zakas, '04

Prayer for the Notre Dame Dorm Community

Dear Lord, may our dorm community
always be filled with your light and love.

In the midst of the physical and emotional pain
we are called to embrace,
send your Holy Spirit
to comfort and accompany us on our spiritual journey
while residing here at our beloved Notre Dame.

In those times we yearn for the loving embrace of our own
    mother,
send Mary, the mother of Jesus, to hold us in her arms,
as only a mother can do.

And when our Notre Dame brothers and sisters
feel a deep emptiness within,
use us as your instruments
to fill them with your joy and peace which never ends.
In gratitude for all God's graces.
> **Linda S. Cirillo**
> **Former Rector, Lewis Hall**

A Child's Summer Vacation Prayer

No more homework, no more tests.
No more getting up for school.
No more book reports or studying.
My summer vacation begins today!
I'm so happy and I'm so free.
I want to read and get up late.
I want to ride my bike and swim.
I want to play more with my friends.

Please bless my summer days, dear God.
Keep me safe and happy.
Catherine Odell

Prayer for Balance

Lord, help me to create a balanced life.
Help me to take time to enjoy life,
to be a person full of gratitude.
Help me take time to love,
to extend my hand in service to those around me.
Lord, remind me to take time to learn,
to be disciplined and accountable.
Help me to make a difference in the
small and big moments of my life.
Lord, help me to keep smiling,
to be happy and true to myself.
Lord, infuse me with your spirit
so I can create a life of balance,
moderation, and simplicity.
And whatever my challenge,
let it be an occasion to deepen my life's purpose.
Susan Burke, '87 MBA

Prayer

Lord, give us the ambition
to do as much as we can,
as well as we can,
as long as we can,
and the resolve not to despair
over the things we cannot do.
Theodore M. Hesburgh, C.S.C.

6

LORD, HEAR OUR PRAYER

Prayers for Times of Struggle

NOTRE DAME
✤ STADIUM ✤

The sisters of Notre Dame preached to me when I was in grade school that God is everywhere. No place is that more evident to me than at the University of Notre Dame. God's presence permeates the campus. I am not referring just to the Basilica of the Sacred Heart or the Grotto, but to the football stadium as well.

I often felt, during a critical stage of a close football game, that more people in the stadium were praying to God than in most churches on Sunday morning, even though they were praying to God for different reasons.

I felt, and still do, that the stadium is a sacred place. Our players would go from our team Mass at Sacred Heart directly to the stadium. After warm-up we would pray the Our Father and the Hail Mary led by our team priest, Jim Riehle, C.S.C. We often asked our football players to conduct their activities both on and off the field according to the Book of Proverbs.

God is always with us wherever we go, and that includes the football field. On my game plan, which I always put in a manila folder, I would always list four of my favorite Bible verses, such as, "Trust in the Lord with all your heart and lean not on your own understanding" (Prv 3:5), or "If God is for me, who can be against me?" (Rom 8:31).

It also says in the Bible that when two or more come together to pray, God will be among them. The sisters were right.

Lou Holtz
Head Football Coach, 1986–1996

✣ TALKING TO GOD ✣

I am a Catholic. I believe in God, and I believe in the power of prayer. However, I have never really been one for structured prayer. That's not to say that I don't give thanks to God for the blessings I've been given, or that I don't offer up a quick prayer when I—or someone I love—is in need of God's protection. But I had never been one to truly set aside time to make a conscious decision to connect with God. Though I was raised a Catholic and have always been taught to pray, the act itself always felt foreign to me.

I thought praying would get easier for me once I came to work at Notre Dame. After all, here you have your pick of sacred spaces where you can sit in peace and share your thoughts with God. I tried sitting in the Basilica of the Sacred Heart and praying, but I found myself getting too distracted by the beautiful murals and statues. I tried the Grotto, but felt I didn't know what to say when I was there. I tried walking around the lakes, and while I enjoyed it, I never really felt the power of God with me when I was there. So what was wrong with me? Why couldn't I pray?

Then it happened. I faced a point when many of the major facets of my life were in turmoil at the same time: the disintegration of the forty-three-year marriage of a couple very close to me; the moving in of a family member with me; a move into a new home; a break-up with a significant relationship; a health scare.

I turned to my mother for support. She gave what she could but also recommended that I "give my problems to God." I didn't know what that meant or how to do it, I told her. "Sometimes," she told me, "all you have to do is tell God you cannot handle the burden you carry, and ask him to take the load."

So that's how it started. One chilly November evening I went back down to the Grotto, lit a candle, told God that I was at my breaking point, and asked him for one thing: "Lord, please let there be peace in my heart." I was not asking God to fix my problems or to remove the burdens, but to fill my heart with peace to accept my situation. All I wanted at that moment was relief from suffering.

I'd like to say that the relief was immediate, but it wasn't. Though my problems weren't instantly erased, I did feel—for the first time—that they wouldn't crush me. This was progress.

So the next day I went to the Grotto and said the same prayer. This continued for several weeks, and soon these sessions turned into conversations. As I grew more and more connected to these conversations with God, I found I didn't always need to schedule them at the Grotto. I began talking to him whenever I felt the need to get something off my chest. I even began talking to God whenever I felt particularly grateful for an outcome in a situation or when I felt happy for no good reason. Those were the best prayers, when I could just say, "Thank you God, for this moment of peace and contentment in my life. I know every day will not be this way, but I am thankful that this one is."

The more I talked to God, the more I realized that praying doesn't need to have a structure or a theme. It doesn't need to be the Hail Mary or the Our Father to count. God listens to all our prayers, no matter what the format.

I still go to the Grotto on occasion, though not every day. And I still walk the lakes at Notre Dame. And every time I do, instead of lamenting at the lack of closeness I feel to God, I relish the casual nature of my relationship with him now. I know that no matter where I am and no matter what I have to say, I have faith my prayers will be heard. And now I make it a point to say a little prayer every day.

Angela Sienko
Notre Dame Alumni Association

PRAYERS FOR TIMES OF STRUGGLE

Do not be afraid, I am with you.
—Jeremiah 1:8

Perhaps nothing drives us into the arms of God as much as suffering. Who else understands our pain? Who else can take our anger? Who else can offer comfort—or at least constant presence—until we find peace and understanding? Though the mystery of suffering has confounded believers and nonbelievers alike since time began, Catholics believe that God is with us in our suffering, not the cause of it. No struggle is too small to take to God in prayer.

We Did Not Want It Easy, God

We did not want it easy, God,
but we did not contemplate
that it would be quite this hard,
this long, this lonely.

So, if we are to be turned inside out,
and upside down,
with even our pockets shaken,
just to check what's rattling
and left behind,
we pray that you will keep faith with us,
and we with you.
Hold our hands as we weep,
giving us strength to continue,
and showing us beacons
along the way
to becoming new.
Anna McKenzie

Pain and Comfort

Interesting life this life. . . .
We are put in places for reasons we can never know—
we are called to be for others rather than for ourselves.
It is not our pain that is the purpose, but the pain of others—
it is not our comfort,
but the comfort of others to whom we are directed.
Lord, let my pain teach me to comfort others.
Bob Sylvester, C.S.C.
Institute for Church Life

To the Great Questioner

It seems to me, Lord
that we search much too desperately for answers,
when a good question holds as much grace as an answer.
Jesus, you are the Great Questioner.

Keep our questions alive,
that we may always be seekers rather than settlers.
Guard us well from the sin of settling in
with our answers hugged to our breasts.
Make of us a wondering, far-sighted, questioning, restless people,
and give us the feet of pilgrims on this journey unfinished.
Macrina Wiederkehr, O.S.B.

Be at Peace

Have no fear for what tomorrow may bring.
The same loving God who cares for you today
will take care of you tomorrow and every day.
He will either shield you from suffering
or give you unfailing strength to bear it.
Be at peace, then,
and put aside all anxious thoughts and imaginations.
St. Francis de Sales

Grotto Prayer

I come here because my heart hurts,
but in this dark cave I can feel the warmth
and presence of all who come before you.
I join my prayers with theirs
and ask for your intercession.
May water spring forth from what seems barren.
May my soul say "Yes" to whatever God asks.
And may this darkness, lit by faith alone,
become the womb that brings forth new life.
Kathleen Healy, '10 MDiv

Prayer after Suicide

Crucified Savior,
there is no place for me to go
but to the foot of your cross.
I feel desolation, defeat, betrayal, rejection.
I tried to stop the flood, to calm the earthquake, to put out the
    raging fire.
I did not even know how desperate it all was.
There is absolutely no consolation, no answer, no softening of
    my grief.
It is complete darkness.
I grieve for my dear friend for what was and what would have
    been.
Is life so awful that all that struggle had to end, that defeat was
    inevitable?
There is nothing but silence outside and screaming inside.
I know that the wound will heal, but now I don't even want it to.
I know that there will be a huge scar in its place.
That scar will be all I have left. . . .

We have no place to go in the world, in the whole universe
but here to you, to your cross—it is our only hope.
   Benedict Groeschel, C.F.R. (abridged)

Prayer for Those with HIV/AIDS

God of our weary years,
God of our silent tears,
O good and gracious God,
you are the God of health and wholeness.
In the plan of your creation,
you call us to struggle in our sickness

and to cling always to the cross of your Son.
O God, we are your servants.

Many of us are now suffering with HIV or AIDS.
We come before you and ask you,
if it is your holy will,
to take this suffering away from us.
Restore us to health and lead us to know you
and your powerful healing love
of body and spirit.
We ask you also
to be with those of us who nurse your sick ones.
We are the mothers, fathers, sisters, brothers,
children, and friends of your suffering people.

It is so hard for us to see those whom we love suffer.
You know what it is to suffer.
Help us to minister in loving care, support, and patience
for your people who suffer with HIV and AIDS.
Lead us to do whatever it will take
to eradicate this illness from the lives of those
who are touched by it,
both directly and indirectly.
Trusting in you and the strength of your Spirit,
we pray these things in the name of Jesus.
  National African American Catholic
  HIV/AIDS Task Force

Prayer for a Sick Child

O most beloved St. Gerard,
who, like the Savior, loved children
and by your prayers freed many from disease and even death,
listen to us who are pleading for our sick child.

We thank God for the great gift of our son/daughter
and ask God to restore our child to health if such be thy holy
　will.
This favor we beg of you through your love for all children and
　mothers.

For Those with Cancer

Bless, O God,
all who struggle with cancer.
Empower them with hope
for each and every day.
Provide them with loving
and tender care, laughter,
and the support of love.
Grant them
courage when they are afraid,
comfort when they are in pain,
and your blessing
when all else seems hopeless,
that in their fight with illness
they may continue to praise you
and glorify your name.
Vienna Cobb Anderson

Blessing for Cancer Treatment

Blessed are you, Compassionate One,
For giving me these droplets
of [*name of chemotherapy drug or radiation treatment*].
Like refreshing dew and healing rain, may they save my life.
Diann L. Neu

A Couple's Prayer to Heal a Hurt

Dear God of unconditional and infinite love,
we apprehensively approach you for healing grace
at a time of tension and distance.
We don't know how you can do it;
let us choose to trust that you can.

We feel disillusioned and lonely even though we are physically
    together.
Our hurts invite us to individual pity parties
where the only guests are emptiness and despair.
Stifle our inclinations to strike out with words and actions
that build an even higher wall between us.

Inspire us to find ways to start the healing process—
ways that build up rather than tear down.
Remind us that if we approach this situation as a contest of wills
and we try to make each other the "loser,"
we will be living with a loser.
Help us to use words that seek understanding,
rebuild commitment, and reflect back to each other
the goodness that we each see and experience.

Strengthen us to work things out as quickly and completely as
    possible
rather than letting them fester and scab.
Don't let us settle for "I'm sorry," which is "me" oriented;
inspire us instead to ask for and grant forgiveness.
Remind us that in the Our Father
we ask you to forgive us as we forgive others.
Renew our realization of each other's qualities that we found so
    attractive.

Let us hunger for a refreshing of our relationship
as we trust that when you brought us together for life,

✠ ────────────────

you knew what you were doing.
May our love somehow increase
as a sparkling sign of your love for the Church.
We may not be able to even imagine how you can do this—
but please surprise us Lord!
> **Kevin and Kathy Misiewicz**
> **Mendoza College of Business**

We tell each other that we are not alone,
that Jesus Christ lives among us.
It gives us courage.
Edward Sorin, C.S.C.
Founder of the University of Notre Dame

Prayer for Natural Disaster

As the storm beats down on the weary and disparaged,
we pray and open our hearts,
our minds, and our faith in God.
We trust that we can make things better.
The weary and disparaged are worthy of our help,
as God is worthy of our love.
And though the storm is heavy,
with God's love as our protection and relief
the storm will be overshadowed by the brighter days ahead.
> **Itiyopiya Ewart**

Prayer for Those Who Cause Suffering

(Found at the side of a dead child in Ravensbruck concentration camp, 1945)

O Lord,
Remember not only the men and women of goodwill,

✠

But all those of ill will.
But do not remember all the suffering
they have inflicted upon us;
remember the fruits we have bought thanks to this suffering:
our comradeship, our loyalty, our humility,
our courage, our generosity,
the greatness of heart which has grown out of all this.
And when they come to judgment,
let all the fruits we have borne
be their forgiveness.

*With all my heart I pardon those who have
persecuted me, and I wish them well.*
Blessed Basile Moreau, C.S.C.
Founder of the Congregation of Holy Cross

Prayer to Overcome Depression

Just as day declines to evening,
so often my heart declines into depression.
Everything seems dull, every action feels like a burden.
If anyone speaks, I scarcely listen.
If anyone knocks, I scarcely hear.
My heart is as hard as flint.

Then I go out into the field to meditate,
to read the holy scriptures,
and I write down my deepest thoughts in a letter to you.
And suddenly your grace, dear Jesus,
shatters the darkness with daylight,
lifts the burden, relieves the tension.
Soon tears follow sighs,
and heavenly joy floods over me with the tears.
            Aelred of Rievaulx

Prayer for Healing

O Lord, my God,
I cried out to you,
and you healed me.
Psalm 30:2

Lead, Kindly Light

Lead, Kindly Light, amid the encircling gloom
    lead thou me on!
The night is dark, and I am far from home—
    lead thou me on!
Keep thou my feet; I do not ask to see
the distant scene—one step enough for me.

I was not ever thus, nor pray'd that thou
    shouldst lead me on.
I loved to choose and see my path, but now
    lead thou me on!
I loved the garish day, and, spite of fears,
pride ruled my will: remember not past years.

So long thy power hath blest me, sure it still
    will lead me on,
O'er moor and fen, o'er crag and torrent, till
    the night is gone;
and with the morn those angel faces smile
which I have loved long since, and lost awhile.
John Henry Newman

Prayer against Anxiety and Depression

Lord, when all is darkness and we feel our weakness and
    helplessness,
give us the sense of your presence, your love, and your strength.
Help us to have perfect trust in your protecting love.
Bless us with your strengthening power
so nothing may frighten or worry us.
We trust that in living close to you,
we shall see your hand, your purpose, your will through all
    things.
    St. Ignatius of Loyola

Prayer to St. Jude for Hopeless Causes

Oh glorious apostle St. Jude,
faithful servant and friend of Jesus,
the name of the traitor who delivered the beloved Master
into the hands of his enemies has caused thee to be forgotten by
    many,
but the Church honors and invokes thee universally
as the patron of hopeless cases—of things despaired of.

Pray for me who am so miserable;
make use, I implore you, of that particular privilege accorded you
of bringing visible and speedy help where help is almost
    despaired of.
Come to my assistance in this great need,
that I may receive the consolations and succor of heaven
in all my necessities, tribulations, and sufferings,
particularly [*mention your request*],
and that I may bless God with you and all the elect throughout
    eternity.

I promise you, O blessed St. Jude, to be ever mindful of this
    great favor,
and I will never cease to honor you as my special and powerful
    patron,
and to do all in my power to encourage devotion to you.

God Alone

Let nothing disturb you.
Let nothing frighten you.
All things are passing;
God only is changeless.
Patience gains all things.
Who has God wants nothing.
God alone suffices.
    St. Teresa of Avila

Lord, not you, it is I who am absent.
Denise Levertov

We Can Handle It

Lord help me to remember
that nothing is going to happen
to me today that you and I
together can't handle.

Be Not Afraid

The Lord is my light and my salvation;
whom shall I fear?
The Lord is the stronghold of my life;
of whom shall I be afraid?
Psalm 27:1

Blessing (*Beannacht*)

On the day when
the weight deadens
on your shoulders
and you stumble,
may the clay dance
to balance you.
And when your eyes
freeze behind
the grey window
and the ghost of loss
gets in to you,
may a flock of colors,
indigo, red, green,
and azure blue
come to awaken in you
a meadow of delight.

When the canvas frays
in the currach of thought
and a stain of ocean
blackens beneath you,
may there come across the waters

a path of yellow moonlight
to bring you safely home.

May the nourishment of the earth be yours,
may the clarity of light be yours,
may the fluency of the ocean be yours,
may the protection of the ancestors be yours.
And so may a slow
wind work these words
of love around you,
an invisible cloak
to mind your life.
John O'Donohue

Balm in Gilead

There is a balm in Gilead
to make the wounded whole;
there is a balm in Gilead
to heal the sin-sick soul.

Some times I feel discouraged,
and think my work's in vain,
but then the Holy Spirit
revives my soul again.

There is a balm in Gilead
to make the wounded whole;
there is a balm in Gilead
to heal the sin-sick soul.

If you can't preach like Peter,
if you can't pray like Paul,
just tell the love of Jesus,
and say He died for all.

✛

There is a balm in Gilead
to make the wounded whole;
there is a balm in Gilead
to heal the sin-sick soul.
African American Spiritual

Give Me Strength

O Holy Spirit, beloved of my soul, I adore you.
Enlighten me, guide me, strengthen me, console me.
Tell me what I should do; give me your orders.
I promise to submit myself to all that you desire of me
and to accept all that you permit to happen to me.
Let me only know your will.
Attributed to Cardinal Désiré-Joseph Mercier

Marisa's Prayer

O Lord, in all that I do and in all that happens,
let me never lose hope.
Let me never think that you have forsaken me;
let me never think that meaning is gone from my life.
Whatever may be, let me trust that you are with me.
Whatever may be, let me not turn away from you,
as you do not turn away from me.
Although your ways are mysterious,
may I believe that your ways will always lead me
to the places I ought to be.
Let me understand enough of the trail
that I may follow you,
wherever that trail may go.
Marisa Anne Lupica (1989–2004)
Daughter of Cindy Elshoff Lupica, '80

Surrender

Receive, O God, the offering of my entire being.
Wholeheartedly, I give you all my will, all my freedom,
all my desires and all my deepest aspirations.
May my whole person, all that is mine,
be put evermore at the service of your Will.
I ask you:
to cleanse my humanity,
to purify my intentions,
and to refine my affectivity in the crucible of your heart.

May this passion for life which I carry within
be transformed always more into love
that is gratuitous, faithful, oriented
and put at your service.
Grant me your Grace, your Love and your Wisdom.
I ask for nothing more.
I let go and freely offer my life to you, saying:
"Here I am God,
I have come to do your will" (Ps 40:7–8).
    Raymonde Maisonneuve, C.S.C.

Serenity Prayer

God grant us the serenity to accept the things we cannot change,
courage to change the things we can,
wisdom to know the difference,
patience for the things that take time,
appreciation for all that we have,
tolerance for those with different struggles,
the freedom to live beyond the limitations of our past ways,
the ability to feel your love for us and our love for each other,

and the strength to get up and try again
even when we feel it's hopeless.
Attributed to Reinhold Niebuhr

There stood by the Cross of Jesus his mother Mary,
who knew grief and was a Lady of Sorrows. She
is our special patroness, a woman who bore much
she could not understand and who stood fast.
Constitution Eight
of the Congregation of Holy Cross

My Boat Is So Small

Dear Lord, be good to me.
The sea is so wide
and my boat is so small.
Breton/Irish Fisherman's Prayer

Buddhist Prayer

May all beings everywhere plagued with sufferings of body and
     mind
quickly be freed from their illnesses.
May those frightened cease to be afraid,
and may those bound be free.
May the powerless find power,
and may people think of befriending one another.

Blessing for Women in Transition

[*Name*], you are a beloved child of God,
fearfully and wonderfully made.

May you listen closely to God's quiet voice
as it guides you on your path.

I pray for all good things to come your way
and I ask God to bless you
and strengthen you
until we meet again.
Jane Leyden Cavanaugh, '85

All Shall Be Well

All shall be well,
and all shall be well,
and all manner of thing shall be well.
St. Julian of Norwich

Feeling Hope after Suffering

I suffered, and now there is joy,
I was lonely, and now there is comfort,
I was desolate, and now there is warmth,
I was empty, and now there is fullness.

This will not last forever.
But thank you, God, for living again,
for letting me know and feel,
your life and presence in me.

⊹

And if this hope should die again,
Let me remember the years of emptiness that passed.
Stay now, God, a little longer.
Edwina Gateley

The Game of Life

Dear Lord,
in the struggle that goes on through life,
we ask for a field that is fair,
a chance that is equal with all the strife,
the courage to strive and to dare;
and if we should win, let it be by the code,
with our faith and our honor held high;
and if we should lose, let us stand by the road
and cheer as the winners go by.
Knute Rockne

7

NOW THANK WE ALL OUR GOD

Prayers of Thanksgiving and Gratitude

TOUCHDOWN JESUS MOSAIC

The north windows of my environmental-justice seminar room looked right out at Millard Sheets's fourteen-story mosaic of Christ the teacher. Students christened this Hesburgh Library monument "Touchdown Jesus," but one class taught me it had another meaning, "Jesus the embracer."

Mostly senior premeds or science majors, my eighteen environmental-justice students were razor sharp. After several weeks, however, I was concerned about one. An African American grandmother, Georgia, lived on the South Side of Chicago. Taking the course on a special tuition-free arrangement, she hoped to learn enough to protect her impoverished community from the ravages of some of the worst pollution in the country. I could see she was struggling.

After class, I asked Georgia how I could help. Her eyes welled with tears, then she smiled. "Every single member of our seminar has contacted me privately and offered to help. I've never known anyone like these students."

The other students never revealed how each had quietly reached out to Georgia. Later I discovered that she was returning these embraces. Concerned that out-of-state premed students would have to go through Northwestern University and the University of Chicago medical school interviews alone, Georgia offered to travel with them, wait outside each interview room as "family," and pray for them. Some took her up on it.

For Jesus the embracer, there is no "we" and "they." Especially at Notre Dame.

Arms reaching out, my seminar students showed they had learned the new lesson of the mosaic. They knew Cesar Chavez was right: all learning is for service.

Kristin Shrader-Frechette
Center for Environmental Justice and Children's Health

✣ GOD BLESS YOU ✣

I t just so happens that two important milestones in my life have coincided with two very special blessings. Not just blessings in the sense of good fortune or abundance, as the word is often used, but literal, spoken prayers of blessing.

The day after my husband and I got engaged on a Lake Michigan beach, we drove to South Bend, my husband's hometown, to share our good news with his parents. We later stopped by the Notre Dame campus, paying a visit to the Grotto to light a candle in honor of our new life as an engaged couple.

As we stood at the Grotto, I caught a glimpse of a familiar face out of the corner of my eye. Lighting a candle next to us was Father Ted Hesburgh. We greeted him and shared with him our happy news. He kindly congratulated us and asked, "Well, is there a ring?" I held out my left hand, my new diamond sparkling in the sunlight. Father Ted blessed my engagement ring and wished us well. I couldn't have asked for a more auspicious beginning to our engagement.

Several years later, shortly after I began working at Notre Dame's Kroc Institute for International Peace Studies, I again crossed paths with Father Ted, at a picnic celebrating the start of the academic year. Seven months pregnant with my first child, I was starting to feel some anxiety about impending childbirth and parenthood. At the urging of my boss, I asked Father Ted to bless me and my daughter. He graciously obliged. I don't remember his exact words, but I remember feeling somehow better prepared for the road ahead by that fleeting, but grace-filled, encounter.

The tradition of blessing people, objects, places—even pets— is as old as creation itself. The book of Genesis tells us that God immediately blessed all that he created: "God looked at everything he had made, and he found it very good" (Gn 1:31). Jesus regularly said prayers of blessing upon the people he healed and, of course, blessed bread and wine before he shared it at the first Eucharist.

To bless something is simply to call forth God's goodness upon an object, a person, or a place. It is not done for the purpose of making something or someone holy, since all that God has created is already good and holy. Rather, blessings call forth special graces and affection from God upon whatever or whomever is being blessed. Also, these blessings help us to better see our surroundings through the lens of faith.

We treasure things that have belonged to deceased grandparents or friends because we sense their presence in their belongings. In the same way, we sense God's presence in a special way in something that has been blessed. Often those objects are religious articles, but they may also be things like tools, cars, food, or houses.

Blessings on people, too, can be given at any time. They seem especially appropriate, however, as one faces a crisis or challenge. They also are especially appropriate during a time when one crosses a threshold, whether between stages of life or geographic locales.

Prayers of blessing are often accompanied by a sprinkle of holy water, the imposition of hands, a kiss, or the Sign of the Cross. More important than the actual gesture is the way that it should be done: slowly, mindfully, reverently. Whenever we pray a blessing, we pray in union with the Church—all the People of God. Whatever we may lack in faith or in fortitude is bolstered by the global community of faith.

While we may be more familiar with blessings being bestowed by clergy, blessing prayers can be prayed by anyone who is baptized. As a new parent, I'm now mindful that it's especially appropriate for parents to bless their children. For me, blessing my daughter each night has become an unexpected but cherished new form of prayer.

No matter how exhausted I might be, I can muster the energy to trace the Sign of the Cross on my daughter's forehead in her crib, and simply to say: God bless and keep you, little one. While in the past I've been on the receiving end of some special blessings, I'm conscious that it's now time to begin bestowing my own, too.

Renée LaReau, '96, '00 MDiv
Kroc Institute for International Peace Studies

PRAYERS OF
✦ THANKSGIVING ✦
AND GRATITUDE

Let the word of Christ dwell in you richly
as you teach and admonish one another with all wisdom,
and as you sing psalms, hymns, and spiritual songs
with gratitude in your hearts to God.
—Colossians 3:16

Let us give thanks to the Lord our God." This invitation from the priest is part of the dialogue that begins the Eucharistic Prayer at Mass. In fact the word *Eucharist* literally means "thanksgiving." But Mass is not the only occasion to express gratitude to God. We are often moved to give thanks after an answered prayer, in response to specific blessings, or in awe of God's creation. We also should remember to thank God daily. An "attitude of gratitude" can give perspective when life is difficult and help cultivate a more optimistic view of life, in a world that is sometimes cynical.

Prayer of Gratitude

O God, when I have food,
help me to remember the hungry;
when I have work,
help me to remember the jobless;
when I have a home,
help me to remember those who have no home at all;
when I am without pain,
help me to remember those who suffer.
And remembering,
help me to destroy my complacency,
bestir my compassion,
and be concerned enough to help,
by word and deed, those who cry
out for what we take for granted.
    Samuel F. Pugh

Native American Prayer

Give thanks
for unknown blessings
already on their way.

Child's Prayer of Thanks

Thank you for the world so sweet.
Thank you for the things we eat.
Thank you for the birds that sing.
Thank you, God, for everything.

✛

Give Thanks

O give thanks to the Lord, for he is good,
for his steadfast love endures for ever.
O give thanks to the God of gods,
for his steadfast love endures for ever.
O give thanks to the Lord of lords,
for his steadfast love endures for ever;
who alone does great wonders,
for his steadfast love endures for ever;
who by understanding made the heavens,
for his steadfast love endures for ever;
who spread out the earth on the waters,
for his steadfast love endures for ever;
who made the great lights,
for his steadfast love endures for ever;
the sun to rule over the day,
for his steadfast love endures for ever;
the moon and stars to rule over the night,
for his steadfast love endures for ever.
   Psalm 136:1–9

Absolution

God forgives you.
Forgive others;
forgive yourself.
   New Zealand Prayer Book

Prayer for Thanksgiving Day

Dear Lord,
bless this gathering of loved ones,
and help us to be ever thankful
for your bountiful blessings
now and throughout the year.

Let this feast remind us of our duty
to the well-being of others.
Guide us in serving faithfully and selflessly
those in need.

We ask that your presence
increase our gratitude
for the care, companionship, and comfort
that our friends and family provide.
And may we always remember
that our relationships in this world
are but a reflection
of your never-ending love.

Julie Schuetz Hipp, '94, '96 MA

Psalm of Thanksgiving

May God be gracious to us and bless us
and make his face to shine upon us,
that your way may be known upon earth,
your saving power among all nations.

Let the peoples praise you, O God;
let all the peoples praise you.
Let the nations be glad and sing for joy,
for you judge the peoples with equity

✤

and guide the nations upon earth.
Let the peoples praise you, O God;
let all the peoples praise you.

The earth has yielded its increase;
God, our God, has blessed us.
May God continue to bless us;
let all the ends of the earth revere him.
Psalm 67

*Once more, we felt that Providence had been
good to us and we blessed God
from the depths of our soul.*
Edward Sorin, C.S.C.
Founder of the University of Notre Dame

Gratitude for Family

Gracious God,
thank you for the family that surrounds me in this earthly life.
Help us to honor each other with love and tenderness.
Give us the courage to forgive one another
when we are hurt or betrayed.
Give us the desire to help each other walk the path of human
    life.
Give us the willingness to bear each other's burdens,
share each other's laughter,
and give each other space and room to grow.
When we look into each other's eyes,
or touch one another's hearts,
help us see your presence and bow with gratitude and awe.
I ask this for the sake of your love.
Renee Miller

Buddhist Prayer of Thanksgiving

Let us rise up and be thankful,
for if we didn't learn a lot today,
at least we learned a little,
and if we didn't learn a little,
at least we didn't get sick,
and if we got sick,
at least we didn't die;
so let us all be thankful.
Attributed to the Buddha

All Good Things Come from You

Lord, you are to be blessed and praised;
all good things come from you:
you are in our words and in our thoughts,
and in all that we do.
St. Teresa of Avila

Gratitude for Friends

Gracious God,
I ask your blessing on all my friends
who have given of their own heart and soul
to deepen and strengthen my own.
I pray especially for those who have walked alongside me
when I have not been a faithful friend myself.
When I feel alone, remind me that my friends
are one of your greatest gifts of grace to me.
Let me be to them what they are to me.
I ask this for the sake of your love.
Renee Miller

Day by Day

Thank you, Lord Jesus Christ,
for all the benefits and blessings
which you have given me,
for all the pains and insults
which you have borne for me.
Merciful friend, Brother, and Redeemer,
may I know you more clearly,
love you more dearly,
and follow you more nearly,
day by day.
St. Richard of Chichester

Gratitude for Gift of Sexuality

Loving God, source of all truth and strength, help me to come to
know you more fully through a greater awareness of myself and
those closest to me.

I know that through loving others I can come to a greater
awareness of your presence by entering into the challenges and
joys of a healthy relationship. Be with me as I strive to be open to
your great mystery in my life and in the lives of those I love.

As I try to understand the great gift of my sexuality, help me to
be true to what is deepest in my heart. Give me the patience to
be still and listen for your voice in the depths of my being.

Then, help me to express this gift, with all of its mystery, in
accord with what is true within me. Grant me the strength to
resist the pressures from others when it is not in keeping with
your will for me.

May my need for emotional intimacy not overshadow an honest decision about what I want to say physically. I know that in choosing to remain true to myself, I am also being truthful to you and those I love so dearly.

Gracious God, be with me in times of doubt. Help me to express my true giftedness in all of my choices and actions.
Darrell R. Paulsen, '94 MDiv
Campus Ministry

If the only prayer you said in your whole life was
"thank you," that would suffice.
Meister Eckhart

Simple Gifts

'Tis the gift to be simple, 'tis the gift to be free,
'tis the gift to come down where we ought to be,
and when we find ourselves in the place just right,
'twill be in the valley of love and delight.
Joseph Brackett

We Thank Thee

For flowers that bloom about our feet,
Father, we thank thee.
For tender grass so fresh, so sweet,
Father, we thank thee.
For the song of bird and hum of bee,
for all things fair we hear or see,
Father in heaven, we thank thee.
For blue of stream and blue of sky,

Father, we thank thee.
For pleasant shade of branches high,
Father, we thank thee.
For fragrant air and cooling breeze,
for beauty of the blooming trees,
Father in heaven, we thank thee.
For this new morning with its light,
Father, we thank thee.
For rest and shelter of the night,
Father, we thank thee.
For health and food, for love and friends,
for everything thy goodness sends,
Father in heaven, we thank thee.

Attributed to Ralph Waldo Emerson

Prayer does not change God, but it changes the one who prays it.
Søren Kierkegaard

Richly Blessed

I asked for strength that I might achieve;
I was made weak that I might learn humbly to obey.
I asked for health that I might do greater things;
I was given infirmity that I might do better things.
I asked for riches that I might be happy;
I was given poverty that I might be wise.
I asked for power that I might have the praise of men;
I was given weakness that I might feel the need of God.
I asked for all things that I might enjoy life;
I was given life that I might enjoy all things.
I got nothing that I had asked for,
but everything that I had hoped for.

Almost despite myself my unspoken prayers were answered;
I am, among all men, most richly blessed.
An unknown Confederate soldier

Gratitude for Grandchildren

Heavenly Father,
thank you for the privilege
of being a grandparent.
You have blessed my life
with precious grandchildren
and I am so grateful.
They make my heart sing
and bring such joy to my life.
I pray that each one will grow up
to live a godly life—
that they will grow with a heart's desire
to know you, love you, and serve you.
Bless and keep them in your loving care.
Be their joy in celebrating achievements,
be their hope on days of discouragement.
Help them to praise you in all things.
Patricia Trost
Notre Dame Alumni Association

Gratitude for Small Things

For a friend's unexpected call,
for a letter unforeseen,
for the sunlight bursting through thick clouds,
for a porpoise frolicking in the water,
for seals basking in the sun,

for an invitation to dinner on a lonely eve,
for a request to "come along";
for all the wonderful surprises of life
we give you thanks, O God of joy.
Vienna Cobb Anderson

Blessed Are You

Blessed are you, loving Father, for all your gifts to us.
Blessed are you for giving us family and friends
to be with us in times of joy and sorrow,
to help us in times of need,
and to rejoice with us in moments of celebration.
St. Teresa of Avila

For Everything

For everything that has been,
Thanks!
For all that is to come,
Yes!
Dag Hammarskjöld

✣ ✣ ✣

8

✣ ✣ ✣

TO
EVERYTHING
THERE IS
A SEASON

Prayers for the Seasons

ST. MARY'S AND
ST. JOSEPH'S LAKES

In 1842, when Father Edward Sorin and his Holy Cross brother companions arrived for the first time at what is now Notre Dame, the deep snow covering and the uncertain boundaries led the viewers to imagine that their new home was adjacent to one large lake. But with the coming of Spring, there were two lakes, newly named St. Mary's and St. Joseph's Lakes. They would become an integral part of the reality of the university as a place of living and study, as a location for prayer and reflection.

Notre Dame's lakes allow the members of the community, as well as the thousands of visitors each year, to decompress, to put things into perspective, to come in touch with nature and with the God of all creation.

Through the cycle of the seasons and according to every meteorological pattern, the lakes reflect the raw beauty of water and clouds, of sun and moon, of trees and shrubs, of ducks, swans, and geese. At a distance, from the rise near the Log Chapel, one can almost imagine the same serene vista in centuries past. Up close, the meandering primitive path girds the two bodies of water as endless streams of humans of every age freely walk and jog and race and enjoy their time.

For those who take the time to look and to listen, it may be that the living God will dazzle with new visions and speak with words of greater clarity, as so many have discovered who have abided here afore.

Edward A. "Monk" Malloy, C.S.C.
President Emeritus of the University of Notre Dame

✢ PRAYER DIRECTIONS ✢

My prayers are mostly little conversations I have with God, but sometimes a good, long talk is important, too, and mine always go best outdoors. As a Notre Dame freshman in 1970 and in the thirty years I have worked on campus, walking the campus lakes has often meant a good heart-to-heart with the Creator.

When I seek these more formal, solitary engagements with God, I use a Native American prayer structure that melds easily with my Catholic disposition.

I start by walking north. The cold, cleansing winds come from there. So I head north and ask these winds to blow through me, to wipe me clear—of preoccupations and nagging thoughts, of anger, grievances, ill will, any festering resentments. I pray for the day's pestering voices to grow silent. Just as winter reduces the landscape to its bare bones, I want a kind of purification. I want to be rid of all that stands between me and God. This is the monk's way, the path of the mindful ascetic.

Honesty is essential to this psychic cleansing. It's important not just to empty the bad, but to fend off worldly distractions and delusions, allures and gratifications. These, too, can be barriers to self-examination, detours in the spiritual journey.

The aim, of course, is to be alone with oneself and with God, and ultimately to be rid of the ego and all that separates us from God and his world so that a kind of communion is attainable.

When I feel that I have reached a happy emptiness and peace, I turn toward the east. The sun rises in the east, bringing the morning light. It carries illumination and redemption. I pray for enlightenment and especially wisdom. Just as spring follows winter, I want an Easter of insight, knowledge, and understanding to flow into me, to fill the dark spaces, to help me see.

I go over the meanings and messages in my life, think them through, ask for insight, intuition, intelligence, and judgment. I pray to see clearly, so that I might go forward with a faithful clarity.

When I have again discerned the plots, characters, and true author of my life story, I bend toward the south. The warm breezes come from the south—the summer winds, the power to grow and bloom, the life-giving breath of the sunbathed season. I pray to love. I pray to nurture, to give, to care for. I pray for those I love and all those whom I should love.

The ultimate measure of a person is his or her ability to love. As I face the south, I ponder all those ways in which I have failed or succeeded to love others, to honor and respect all creation, and I pray to be better.

I then turn to the west. According to the Lakota who taught me this prayer of the four directions, the west is the horizon from which the Thunder Beings come. These are the powerful forces that shake up the universe, hurl lightning, and bang the sky with thunder. So I face west and consider how the Holy Spirit moves in and through my life. This is the hardest of the directions to talk about because its Pentecost sweep is fleeting and mysterious; it defies the articulations of reason. And yet what is more profound, more enduring than these spiritual forces?

These invisible currents are difficult, too, because they unnerve us. They challenge our daily excursions, driving us from society's accepted and familiar pathways. Saying *yes* to the gust of the Spirit might turn a world upside down. And as the four directions are paired to the seasons, the west is autumn, with its sense of impending mortality a reminder of the importance of spiritual cultivation.

When I have aligned my interior landscape with the meanings of the four directions, I pause. Across the road from the Grotto, there by the giant sycamore, on the banks of the spring-fed lake,

I pray, thanking God for life and all the gifts of heaven and earth, Mother Earth and Father Sky. I count my blessings. These directions, too, offer rich texts for contemplation and grace, sanctity, acceptance, harmony, and transcendence.

I make this pilgrimage often. When I do, I ask God to meet me on my way. I have not been let down yet.

Kerry Temple, '74
Notre Dame Magazine

PRAYERS FOR THE SEASONS

And God said, "Let there be lights in the expanse of the sky
to separate the day from the night,
and let them serve as signs to mark
seasons and days and years."
—Genesis 1:14

Seasons give our lives rhythm and meaning. At Notre Dame, there is football season, final exam season, and, of course, the winter season, which seems to last forever. In addition to nature's seasons, the Church also celebrates liturgical seasons: Advent, Christmas, Lent, Easter, and Pentecost. In between those special seasons is Ordinary Time. But isn't it all ordinary? Every year students return to campus, the trees lose their leaves, and Christians mark the feasts that help us remember the life of Jesus. Prayer helps us mark these special—and ordinary—seasons.

A Season for Everything

For everything there is a season,
and a time for every matter under heaven:
a time to be born, and a time to die;
a time to plant, and a time to pluck up what is planted;
a time to kill, and a time to heal;
a time to break down, and a time to build up;
a time to weep, and a time to laugh;
a time to mourn, and a time to dance;
a time to throw away stones, and a time to gather stones
    together;
a time to embrace, and a time to refrain from embracing;
a time to seek, and a time to lose;
a time to keep, and a time to throw away;
a time to tear, and a time to sew;
a time to keep silence, and a time to speak;
a time to love, and a time to hate;
a time for war, and a time for peace.
Ecclesiastes 3:1–8

Let Every Day

Let every day combine
the beauty of spring,
the brightness of summer,
the abundance of autumn,
and the repose of winter.
And at the end of my life on earth,
grant that I may come to see and to know you
in the fullness of your glory.
St. Thomas Aquinas

Autumn Prayer

God of all creation,
You give us the gift of seasons to mark our journey through time.
The season of autumn, with its change of colors and falling
    leaves,
reminds us that sometimes things must die
and fall away for new life to arise.
Such is the message of the cross—
that through death to self we find life in all its richness.
In those moments when we experience setbacks or failures,
help us to remember that you are with us always,
and that there is no failure or sin your love cannot heal.
Help us to trust in you and in your promise of new life.
Peter Jarret, C.S.C.

Hurry then; take up this work of resurrection.
Blessed Basile Moreau, C.S.C.
Founder of the Congregation of Holy Cross

Fall Prayer

I think of the trees
and how simply they let go,
let fall the riches of a season,
how without grief (it seems)
they can let go and go deep into their roots
for renewal and sleep.
May Sarton

✛

Prayer for Autumn Days

God of the seasons,
there is a time for everything;
there is a time for dying and a time for rising.
We need courage to enter into the transformation process.

God of autumn,
the trees are saying goodbye to their green,
letting go of what has been.
We, too, have our moments of surrender,
with all their insecurity and risk.
Help us to let go when we need to do so.

God of fallen leaves lying in colored patterns on the ground,
our lives have their own patterns.
As we see the patterns of our own growth,
may we learn from them.

God of misty days and harvest moon nights,
there is always the dimension of mystery and wonder in our lives.
We always need to recognize your power-filled presence.
May we gain strength from this.

God of harvest wagons and fields of ripened grain,
many gifts of growth lie within the season of our surrender.
We must wait for harvest in faith and hope.
Grant us patience when we do not see the blessings.

God of geese going south for another season,
your wisdom enables us to know what needs to be left behind
and what needs to be carried into the future.
We yearn for insight and vision.

God of flowers touched with frost
and windows wearing white designs,
may your love keep our hearts
from growing cold in the empty seasons.

God of life,
you believe in us, you enrich us,
you entrust us with the freedom to choose life.
For all this, we are grateful.
Joyce Rupp

A Prayer in Winter

Dear Lord, the summer is over and gone,
and the harvest is once more past.
All the wealth and warmth of the summer sun
is marvelously packaged now,
in seed and fruit and vegetable,
and stored away in bins and cribs and basements.

Thank you, dear, generous God,
for all your goodness and for all your gifts.
All summer long you are working for us,
storing heat and health and nourishment in the fields and woods.
Now, when the air is cold, and there is no fruitfulness
    in the earth,
we can live on what the summer
and the harvest have stored up for us.

Help us, too, to store up spiritual wealth in the summer
    of this life,
while we can yet work.
Otherwise life's autumn will come,
death will call us, a spiritual winter will set in

and we shall be found poor and unsheltered
not for one season only, but for the winters of eternity.

Lord, we trust in you, that, cooperating with your many graces,
we may make good use now of our rich opportunities.
And may we then reap a rich spiritual harvest
which we will enjoy with you and your saints
in the eternal spring and summer of heaven.
National Catholic Rural Life Conference

*Prayer is not asking. Prayer is putting oneself
in the hands of God, at his disposition, and
listening to his voice in the depths of our
hearts.*

Blessed Mother Teresa of Calcutta

Prayer for Spring

Lord of the springtime,
Father of flower, field, and fruit,
smile on us in these earnest days
when the work is heavy and the toil wearisome;
lift up our hearts, O God, to the things worthwhile—
sunshine and night, the dripping rain, the song of the birds,
books and music, and the voices of our friends.
Lift up our hearts to these this night and grant us thy peace.
W. E. B. Du Bois

In Praise of Summer

God speaks:
"I am the breeze that nurtures all things green
I am the rain coming from the dew

that causes the grasses to laugh with joy of life.
I am the yearning for good."
Hildegard of Bingen

Prayer for Gardens

Dear mother earth,
who day by day unfolds rich blessing on our way,
O praise God! Alleluia!
The fruits and flowers that verdant grow,
let them his praise abundant show.
O praise God, O praise God, Alleluia, Alleluia, Alleluia.
St. Francis of Assisi

A Prayer for Rain

O God, in whom we live and move and have our being,
grant us rain in due abundance,
that being sufficiently helped with temporal gifts
we may seek with more confidence those that are eternal.
National Catholic Rural Life Conference

Advent Prayer

Come, long-expected Jesus.
Excite in me a wonder
at the wisdom and power of your Father and ours.
Receive my prayer as part of my service of the Lord
who enlists me in God's own work for justice.

Come, long-expected Jesus.
Excite in me a hunger for peace:
peace in the world, peace in my home, peace in myself.

Come, long-expected Jesus.
Excite in me a joy responsive to the Father's joy.
I seek his will so I can serve with gladness, singing, and love.

Come, long-expected Jesus.
Excite in me the joy and love and peace
it is right to bring to the manger of my Lord.
Raise in me, too, sober reverence for the God who acted there,
hearty gratitude for the life begun there,
and spirited resolution to serve the Father and Son.
I pray in the name of Jesus Christ, whose advent I hail.
Catholic Online

The O Antiphons

O Wisdom, coming forth from the mouth of the Most High,
reaching from one end to the other,
mightily and sweetly ordering all things:
Come to teach us the way of prudence.

O Adonai, and leader of the House of Israel,
who appeared to Moses in the fire of the burning bush
and gave him the law on Sinai:
Come to redeem us with an outstretched arm.

O Root of Jesse, standing as a sign among the peoples;
before whom kings will shut their mouths,
whom the nations will implore:
Come to deliver us, and do not now delay.

O Key of David and scepter of the House of Israel;
you open and no one can shut;
you shut and no one can open:
Come and lead the prisoners from the prison house,
those who dwell in darkness and the shadow of death.

O Morning Star,
splendor of light eternal and sun of righteousness:
Come and enlighten those who dwell in darkness and the
    shadow of death.

O King of the nations, and their desire,
the cornerstone making both one:
Come and save the human race,
which you fashioned from clay.

O Emmanuel, our king and our lawgiver,
the hope of the nations and their Savior:
Come to save us, O Lord our God.
The Liturgy of the Hours

Light and Darkness

Lord Jesus,
Master of both the light and the darkness,
send your Holy Spirit upon our preparations for Christmas.
We who have so much to do seek quiet spaces to hear your voice
    each day.
We who are anxious over many things look forward to your
    coming among us.
We who are blessed in so many ways long for the complete joy of
    your kingdom.
We whose hearts are heavy seek the joy of your presence.

We are your people, walking in darkness, yet seeking the light.
To you we say, "Come Lord Jesus!"
Mark Nielsen

Christmas Prayer

Wake up
little baby God,
thousands of children
have been born
just like you,
without a roof,
without bread,
without protection.
Chilean Christmas Card

Blessing of a Christmas Tree

God of light and darkness,
Maker of heaven and earth,
in the deep midwinter you gather us
beneath the tree of life.

Bless all those who gather around this Christmas tree:
May the gifts it shelters make present your heavenly grace.
May the lights it holds lead us to the Light of the World.
And may the color it bears announce your unfailing love,
evergreen in the eternal spring you promise in Jesus Christ,
Emmanuel, God with us,
your Son and our Savior,
now and forever.
Bryan Cones

Ash Wednesday Blessing

From the dust of the earth you were created,
to the dust you return.
Repent and believe the gospel.

> *Without prayer even the most charming solitude*
> *is as land without water, producing*
> *only briars and thorns.*
> **Blessed Basile Moreau, C.S.C.**
> Founder of the Congregation of Holy Cross

Lenten Morning Prayer

God, our liberator,
free us from the chains of selfishness
and the false idols of materialism.
Move us to show regard for the lowly,
advocate for the voiceless,
and rescue victims from their oppressors.
Remove the grind of poverty
by opening our hearts and minds
to your Gospel message to love our neighbor.
Awaken our desires with the gifts of your Spirit,
so your justice may be fulfilled.
In Christ, we make this prayer.
> **William Purcell, '86, '92 MDiv**
> **Center for Social Concerns**

✛ STATIONS OF THE CROSS ✛

The Stations of the Cross trace Jesus' journey to his crucifixion and death. Originally a substitute for pilgrimage to Jerusalem, praying the stations is especially popular on Fridays during Lent. Individuals or groups can meditate before the stations, or pray an Our Father, Hail Mary, and Glory Be or other prayer or reflection. At Notre Dame, students and visitors pray at the outdoor stations around St. Joseph's Lake, at indoor ones in the Basilica of the Sacred Heart or dormitory chapels, or as part of the campus-wide, candle-lit stations procession the Tuesday of Holy Week.

✛ ✛ ✛

Prayers before the Stations

God of power and mercy,
in love you sent your Son
that we might be cleansed of
　sin
and live with you forever.
Bless us as we gather to reflect
on his suffering and death
that we may learn from his
　example
the way we should go.
We ask this through that
　same Christ, our Lord.

Traditional Stations of the Cross

1. Jesus is condemned to death.
2. Jesus is given his cross.
3. Jesus falls the first time.
4. Jesus meets his Mother.
5. Simon of Cyrene carries the cross.
6. Veronica wipes the face of Jesus.
7. Jesus falls the second time.
8. Jesus meets the daughters of Jerusalem.
9. Jesus falls the third time.
10. Jesus is stripped of his garments.
11. Jesus is nailed to the cross.
12. Jesus dies on the cross.
13. Jesus' body is removed from the cross.
14. Jesus is laid in the tomb.

Scriptural Stations of the Cross

1. Jesus in the Garden of Gethsemane.
2. Jesus is betrayed by Judas and arrested.
3. Jesus is condemned by the Sanhedrin.
4. Jesus is denied by Peter.
5. Jesus is judged by Pilate.
6. Jesus is scourged and crowned with thorns.
7. Jesus takes up his cross.
8. Jesus is helped by Simon to carry his cross.
9. Jesus meets the women of Jerusalem.
10. Jesus is crucified.
11. Jesus promises his kingdom to the repentant thief.
12. Jesus entrusts Mary and John to each other.
13. Jesus dies on the cross.
14. Jesus is laid in the tomb.

Prayer after the Stations

Lord Jesus Christ,
your passion and death is the sacrifice that unites earth
    and heaven
and reconciles all people to you.
May we who have faithfully reflected on these mysteries
follow in your steps and so come to share your glory in
heaven where you live and reign with the Father and
the Holy Spirit one God, for ever and ever.

Lenten Psalm of Longing

I thank you, O God,
>   for the warming of the winds
>   that brings a melting of the snow,
>   for daylight hours that daily grow longer
>   and richer in the aroma of hope.
Spring lingers beneath the horizon
>   as approaching echoes of Easter
>   ring in my ears.
I lift up my heart to you, Beloved,
>   in this season of Lent
>   that gently sweeps across
>   my sluggish and sleeping heart,
>   awakening me
>   to a deeper love for you.
May the wind of the Spirit
>   that drove Jesus into the desert,
>   into the furnace of prayer,
>   also drive me with a passion
>   during the Lenten season
>   to enkindle the fire of my devotion
>   in the desert of Lenten love.
Birds above, on migratory wings,
>   signal to an inner migration,
>   a message that draws me homeward bound
>   on Spirit's wings
>   to the heart of my Beloved.
May I earnestly use this Lenten season
>   to answer the inner urge
>   to return.
>   **Edward Hays**

Collect for Holy Thursday

Lord Jesus Christ,
we thank you that in this wonderful sacrament
you have given us the memorial of your passion:
grant us so to reverence the sacred mysteries of your body and
    blood
that we may know within ourselves
and show forth in our lives
the fruits of your redemption;
for you are alive and reign, now and for ever.

Good Friday Prayer before a Crucifix

Who is this who waits
with arms extended
and wide open hands?
It is Christ, Our Lord.

For ages and ages,
he has been waiting here,
generations have passed,
he has not folded his wings
or closed his eyes.

For whom does he wait,
for whom the invitation,
for whom the inexhaustible patience
of infinite love?

It is for one,
who comes slowly,
hesitating, afraid,
trusting more to chance,

to perishable things
and the frailties of men,
than to the everlasting arms.

It is for me,
that for two thousand years,
Love has waited here,
with wide wings spread.
It is for me, the courtesy
that will not be importunate,
will not constrain my love
or force the suit.
It is for me,
the silence of the word
wherein the beating heart
alone is audible.

It is for me that God awaits,
with open hands,
a beggar at the locked gates of my soul.
It is for one who doubts,
mistrusts and fears,
who sees the tears
upon the human face of God,
through her own tears, and is not moved.

Of all the world unworthiest to be loved,
driven at last
from self-inflicted harms,
reluctantly, to the Eternal Arms.
                Caryll Houselander

Prayer for Holy Saturday

May our Lord Jesus Christ, your Son,
who alone by his powerful word governs all things,
yet has buried the shame of the cross and iron bonds,
who has broken the bars of the bronze doors
and has descended into hell,
who has shone with the brightness of a new light
on those who were sitting in the shadow of death—
may he, the sun of justice, rising from the tomb,
shine upon our darkness with the marvelous light of his risen
    body.
    Eileen O'Callaghan

Easter Vigil

This is the night of nights, the night of faith and of hope.
While all is shrouded in darkness, God, the Light, keeps watch.
With him there keep watch all who hope and trust in him.
O Mary, this is truly your night!
As the last lights of the Sabbath are extinguished,
and the fruit of your womb rests in the earth, your heart too
    keeps watch!
Your faith and your hope look ahead.
Behind the heavy stone, they already detect the empty tomb;
behind the thick veil of darkness, they glimpse the dawn of the
    Resurrection.
Grant, O Mother, that we too may keep watch in the silence of
    the night,
believing and hoping in the Lord's word.
Thus shall we meet, in the fullness of light and life, Christ, the
    first-fruits of the risen,

who reigns with the Father and the Holy Spirit, for ever and ever.
Queen of Heaven, rejoice, Alleluia!
Pope John Paul II

Easter Prayer

When we are all despairing;
when the world is full of grief;
when we see no way ahead,
and hope has gone away:
 Roll back the stone.
Although we fear change;
although we are not ready;
although we'd rather weep
and run away:
 Roll back the stone.
Because we're coming with the women;
because we hope where hope is vain;
because you call us from the grave
and show the way:
 Roll back the stone.
 Janet Morley

Ascension Prayer

Blessed are you, God of endless glory,
for the daylight that scatters the darkness of night.
Today Christ is brought to your right hand,
and all creation rejoices at the gift of redemption.
In glory, Jesus ascends to heaven,
bearing to you a redeemed and thankful people
made clean in the blood of the eternal Passover.

All glory and praise be yours
through Christ and the Holy Spirit
forever and ever.

Edward F. Gabriele

Pentecost Prayer to the Holy Spirit

Breathe in me, O Holy Spirit,
that my thoughts may all be holy;
Act in me, O Holy Spirit,
that my work, too, may be holy;
Draw my heart, O Holy Spirit,
that I love but what is holy;
Strengthen me, O Holy Spirit,
to defend all that is holy;
Guard me, then, O Holy Spirit,
that I always may be holy.

St. Augustine

9

THY
KINGDOM
COME

Prayers for the World

THE PEACE
MEMORIAL

⊹ ⊹

The students call it Stonehenge. Some see it as a war memorial. I prefer to look upon it as a peace fountain.

Raised up where once rested the old Field House, enormous pillars of limestone framed with a black marble basin now stand in the spray of high gushing waters.

This fountain of living water is a memorial of the mid-century wars of this country, and its purpose is to keep alive the memory of some five hundred Notre Dame students that have given their lives for the cause of their nation and its people.

No war is anything but tragic. Perhaps World War II comes closest to a "good" war in the eyes of almost everyone, for in that war an unbridled aggression was opposed and overcome. The Asian conflicts of Korea and Vietnam have never been so readily resolved in our national conscience. The moral issues were not as clear.

What does remain clear is this: anyone who lays down his or her life has made a statement that carries a credibility and a generosity that nothing can take away.

Every few months someone puts a box of detergent in the fountain and it becomes a sea of foam. The prank has become tedious, and the soap suds dissolve the oils in the bearings of the water pumps.

I wonder—do we play at life? Surely we thoughtlessly play at war. And not all the soap in the world will wash all the blood off our hands.

Nicholas Ayo, C.S.C.
Professor Emeritus of Liberal Studies

THE VOICE
OF PRAYER

I was on retreat in northern California talking to my director about my prayer life. I was becoming bored with the recitation of the daily Office. It was what spiritual writers term a period of dryness. It had begun to feel like a required exercise, and I was rushing through simply to finish. He pointed out that I was approaching it as an obligation to be fulfilled rather than an opportunity to listen to God speaking through the Psalms. He suggested I slow down and simply stop whenever I encountered a line or verse that struck me.

Two days later I came across Psalm 136: "O give thanks to the Lord, for he is good, for his steadfast love endures for ever." The second part, "for his love endures for ever," repeats itself every other line through nine stanzas. The repetition was overpowering and felt like waves crashing endlessly against a cliff. It is the surety upon which we place all our hope for salvation, and a decade later the resounding chorus of that line still rings in my ears.

My favorite literary insight into prayer confirms that sometimes we talk overly much to God, forgetting that it is about spending time with the one who loves us most. *Hearken Unto the Voice* by Franz Werfel (best known as the author of *The Song of Bernadette*) is a fictionalized account of the prophet Jeremiah's life that begins one morning when he is twenty-one and startled out of sleep by God.

As he is with other Old Testament messengers, God is characteristically stingy with blueprint details as he thrusts a seemingly impossible project upon a bewildered young man. But duly commissioned a prophet, Jeremiah meanders his way to Jerusalem. In a fog as to exactly how his feet have transported him to that spot, Jeremiah ascends to the outdoor pulpit in the temple precincts.

A few lines later, he will channel God's voice, reproaching countrymen blind to their iniquity, but first the author inserts a dramatic pause that portrays him struggling to overcome his fear: "He had only to close his eyes to be more aware of the Lord than he had ever been. But one thing was essential: he must not desperately seek for words or struggle to express his own thoughts. His task was to entrust himself to the Lord as he did when he slept . . . and to empty his senses of himself almost to the verge of dissolution."

After twelve years of Catholic schooling and four more in the seminary, I was well trained in word-prayers. They are helpful ignition switches for jump-starting an ongoing dialog with God, but the more difficult part, as in any conversation, is to be a good listener. It requires finding a quiet place and stilling the mind until only the beating of one's heart is audible. If you've ever sat alone at midnight next to a wilderness lake under a carpet of stars and heard the startle of a fish plop a hundred yards away, you have an idea of what it is like to be fully present to God in prayer, open to the surprises of his revelation.

For Christians who struggle with everything from distraction to evil, the words of the Our Father instruct us how to pray each day: "thy will be done," not mine; "our daily bread," no safety net. Still, we might repeat those phrases fifty-thousand times without realizing that their aim is to compel us, as they did Jeremiah, to empty ourselves to the point of dissolution, and place ourselves entirely in God's hands.

Whatever methods we use—centering prayer, *lectio divina*, Liturgy of the Hours, or sitting in silence on a Grotto bench gazing at the Mother who fully opened her heart to God—attentive prayer is profoundly counterintuitive, humbling, and just plain hard to persevere at without stumbling off track periodically. It is natural to welcome distractions when pressed, and it is easy to drift into thinking ourselves justified merely by putting in the

time. However, that is how we fuel our hunger for the force of his wisdom—by taking some time each day to put aside interruptions, ambitions, worries, and even obligations to hearken unto the Lord's voice—for good conversation is always the product of great listening.

James B. King, C.S.C.
Religious Superior of Holy Cross Priests
and Brothers at Notre Dame

✢

PRAYERS FOR
✣ THE WORLD ✣

Now you are the body of Christ. . . .
If one part suffers, every part suffers.
—1 Corinthians 12:26–27

So often we turn to God in prayer when we are in need, when we have an individual concern or one that affects a family member or close friend. But our Catholic faith also compels us to care about—and to pray for—the concerns of the wider world, especially people who suffer deeply because of poverty, war, famine, natural disaster, or other violence. Catholic social teaching calls this "the preferential option for the poor" and concern for the common good. Our faith also calls us to action in service and justice for the world's hurting, but that action must always be accompanied by prayer.

For Justice and Peace

Almighty and eternal God.
May your grace enkindle in all of us
a love for the many unfortunate people
whom poverty and misery
reduce to a condition of life
unworthy of human beings.

Arouse in the hearts of those who call you Father
a hunger and thirst for social justice
and for fraternal charity
in deeds and in truth.

Grant, O Lord,
peace in our days,
peace to souls,
peace to families,
peace to our country,
and peace among nations.
Pope Pius XII

Prayer for Justice

God of justice and love,
Strengthen our minds and hearts
to believe in ourselves and
to love you more dearly.
Remind us that in caring for your people
we come to know you more deeply.

Provide us with the courage
to seek good for all members
of our community, our nation, our world.

May we walk humbly in this journey
of following your Son's path
of reaching out to those
most in need,
and walking with them in
righting the wrongs of our time.
William Purcell, '86, '92 MDiv
Center for Social Concerns

Prayer for Injustice

O God, we pray for all those in our world
who are suffering from injustice:
for those who are discriminated against
because of their race, color, or religion;
for those imprisoned
for working for the relief of oppression;
for those who are hounded
for speaking the inconvenient truth;
for those tempted to violence
as a cry against overwhelming hardship;
for those deprived of reasonable health and education;
for those suffering from hunger and famine;
for those too weak to help themselves
and who have no one else to help them;
for the unemployed who cry out
for work but do not find it.

We pray for anyone of our acquaintance
who is personally affected by injustice.
Forgive us, Lord, if we unwittingly share in the conditions
or in a system that perpetuates injustice.

✢

Show us how we can serve your children
and make your love practical by washing their feet.
Blessed Mother Teresa of Calcutta

Prayer for Social Justice

God our Mother,
Living Water,
River of Mercy,
Source of Life,
in whom we live and move
and have our being,
who quenches our thirst,
refreshes our weariness,
bathes and washes and cleanses our wounds,
be for us always
a fountain of life,
and for all the world
a river of hope,
springing up in the midst
of the deserts of despair.
Honor and blessings,
glory and praise,
to you forever. Amen.
Miriam Therese Winter

For Those Who Work for Justice

Blessed are those who commit themselves
to the search for a just social order,
to promote those changes of attitudes
that are necessary for those on society's margins

to find a place at the human family's table.
Pope John Paul II

For Those Who Serve

Make us worthy, Lord,
to serve our fellow men throughout the world
who live and die in poverty and hunger.
Give them through our hands this day their daily bread,
and by our understanding grant them love, peace, and joy.
Pope Paul VI

*Our mission sends us across borders of every
sort. Often we must make ourselves at home
among more than one people or culture,
reminding us again that the farther we go in
giving, the more we stand to receive.*

**Constitution Two
of the Congregation of Holy Cross**

A Prayer for Compassion

Spirit of Wisdom,
may we bear your love for humanity
by bringing good news to the poor.
Acting according to your will,
we will come to know your reign
where all will be seated at your heavenly banquet.
Let us bring food to the hungry,
healing to the violated,
and presence to the lonely.

✢

Teach us to shine like the stars
in our relationship with God,
    with our neighbor,
    and with all of creation.
Lead us in promoting peace and integrity
    through our everyday challenges.
May your comforting embrace bring us compassion for others.
    William Purcell, '86, '92 MDiv
    Center for Social Concerns

An Instrument of Your Peace

Lord, make me an instrument of your peace;
where there is hatred, let me sow love;
where there is injury, pardon;
where there is doubt, faith;
where there is despair, hope;
where there is darkness, light;
and where there is sadness, joy.
O Divine Master,
grant that I may not so much seek to be consoled as to console;
to be understood, as to understand;
to be loved, as to love;
for it is in giving that we receive,
it is in pardoning that we are pardoned,
and it is in dying that we are born to eternal life.
    St. Francis of Assisi

Peace Prayers

In the name of Allah, the beneficent, the merciful.
Praise be to the Lord of the Universe
who has created us and made us into tribes and nations
that we may know each other, not that we may despise each
     other.
If the enemy incline towards peace,
do thou also incline towards peace, and trust God,
for God is the one that hears and knows all things.
And the servants of God, most gracious are those
who walk on the earth in humility,
and when we address them, we say, "Peace."
     From the Muslim Tradition

Grant us peace, your most gracious gift, O Eternal Source of
     peace,
and give us the will to proclaim its message to all the people on
     earth.
Bless our country, that it may always be a stronghold of peace,
and its advocate among the nations.
May contentment reign within its borders,
health and happiness within its homes.
Strengthen the bonds of friendship among the inhabitants of all
     lands.
And may the love of your name hallow every home and every
     heart.
     From the Jewish Tradition

May all beings have happiness and the causes of happiness;
may all be free from sorrow and the causes of sorrow;
may all never be separated from the sacred happiness which is
     sorrowless;

⁘

and may all live in equanimity,
without too much attachment and too much aversion,
and live believing in the equality of all that lives.
From the Buddhist Tradition

Om Shanti, shanti, shanti.
(Peace, peace, peace be unto all.)
From the Hindu Tradition

To Love Your Enemies

Oh God, help us in our lives and in all of our attitudes,
to work out this controlling force of love,
this controlling power that can solve
every problem that we confront in all areas.
Oh, we talk about politics;
we talk about the problems facing our atomic civilization.
Grant that all men will come together and discover
that as we solve the crisis and solve these problems,
the international problems,
the problems of atomic energy,
the problems of nuclear energy,
and yes, even the race problem;
let us join together in a great fellowship of love
and bow down at the feet of Jesus.
Give us this strong determination.
Martin Luther King Jr.

Prayer for the Planet

Here we are, God—a planet at prayer.
Attune our spirits, that we may hear your harmonies
and bow before your creative power,
that we may face our violent discords
and join with your Energy to make heard in every heart your
    hymn of peace.

Here we are, God—a militarized planet.
Transform our fears, that we may transform our war fields into
    wheat fields,
arms into handshakes, missiles into messengers of peace.

Here we are, God—a polluted planet.
Purify our vision, that we may perceive ways to purify our
    beloved lands,
cleanse our previous waters, de-smog our life-giving air.

Here we are, God—an exploited planet.
Heal our heart, that we may respect our resources,
hold priceless our people, and provide for our starving children
    an abundance of daily bread.
    Joan Metzner, M.M.

For Protection of Human Life at Its Beginning

God our Father, you lovingly knit us in our mothers' wombs.
Grant that each human embryo will be respected as a human being,
and not dismissed as a product to be manipulated or destroyed.
Grant us the courage and conviction to be your voice
for our sisters and brothers at the very earliest stages of their
    development,
and for all defenseless unborn children.

Jesus, Divine Healer, foster in those conducting medical research
a commitment to finding cures in ways
that respect these little ones and all your vulnerable children.

Holy Spirit, grant us the wisdom to develop morally sound
treatments
for conditions now thought to be incurable.
Help us persevere in defending human life while alleviating
suffering.
Show mercy to all who have cooperated in killing our tiniest
brothers and sisters.
Bring them and all who support destructive embryo research to
true conversion.
Grant them the ability to see the immeasurable dignity of all
human beings,
even in the first days of life.
Father, we ask this in Jesus' name, through the Holy Spirit.
United States Conference of Catholic Bishops

*Dedicate some of your life to others. Your
dedication will not be a sacrifice. It will be
an exhilarating experience because it is an
intense effort applied toward a meaningful
end.*

Thomas A. Dooley

That None Should Be Lost

Almighty and ever-living God,
your will for humanity is that none should be lost,
that all should be saved and find their home in you.
In Jesus, you came among us in poverty and simplicity,
to show us the inherent dignity of each human life,

and to reveal your special love for the poor.
We thank you for entrusting to our care your vulnerable ones.
Let us joyfully celebrate the miracles we witness in our midst,
and help us to rededicate ourselves to continue to extend your
    loving hand
to all those who come our way.
Adapted from the *Sacramentary*

Prayer for the Homeless

O God,
as Naomi and Ruth journeyed from one land to another seeking
    a home,
we ask your blessing upon all who are homeless in this world.
You promised to your chosen people a land flowing with milk
    and honey;
so inspire us to desire the accomplishment of your will
that we may work for the settlement of those who are homeless
in a place of peace, protection, and nurture,
flowing with opportunity, blessing, and hope.
Adapted from Vienna Cobb Anderson

Prayer to End Racism

Good and gracious God,
Who loves and delights in all people,
we stand in awe before you,
knowing that the spark of life within each person on earth
is the spark of your divine life.
Differences among cultures and races
are multicolored manifestations of your Light.
May our hearts and minds be open to celebrate

✢ The Notre Dame Book of Prayer

similarities and differences among our sisters and brothers.
We place our hopes for racial harmony
in our committed action and in your presence in our neighbor.
May all peoples live in peace.
Sisters of Mercy of the Americas

For Immigrant Justice

Blessed are you, Lord God,
King of all creation.
Through your goodness, we live in this land
that you have so richly blessed.
Help us always to recognize our
blessings come from you
and remind us to share them
with others, especially those who come
to us today from other lands.
Help us to be generous, just, and welcoming,
as you have been and are generous to us.
Catholic Campaign for Immigrant Reform

Prayer of the Farm Workers' Struggle

Show me the suffering of the most miserable
so I will know my people's plight.
Free me to pray for others,
for you are present in every person.
Help me take responsibility for my own life
so that I can be free at last.
Grant me courage to serve others,
for in service there is true life.
Give me honesty and patience

✢

192

so that the Spirit will be alive among us.
Let the Spirit flourish and grow
so that we will never tire of the struggle.
Let us remember those who have died for justice,
for they have given us life.
Help us love even those who hate us
so we can change the world.
   Cesar E. Chavez

Pope's Prayer at Hiroshima

To you, Creator of nature and humanity,
in truth and beauty I pray:
Hear my voice, for it is the voice of victims
of all wars and violence among individuals and nations.
Hear my voice, for it is the voice of all children who suffer
and will suffer when people put their faith in weapons and war.

Hear my voice when I beg you to instill
into the hearts of all human beings
the wisdom of peace, the strength of justice,
and the joy of fellowship.
Hear my voice, for I speak for the multitudes in every country
and every period of history who do not want war
and are ready to walk the road of peace.

Hear my voice, and grant insight and strength so that we
may always respond to hatred with love,
to injustice with total dedication to justice,
to need with the sharing of self,
to war with peace.

O God hear my voice, and grant unto the world your everlasting
peace.

Pope John Paul II

Prayer for the Anniversary of 9/11

Come Holy Spirit, breathe down upon our troubled world,
shake the tired foundations of our crumbling institutions,
break the rules that keep you out of all our sacred spaces.
And from the dust and rubble, gather up the seedlings of a new
creation.

Come Holy Spirit, inflame once more the dying embers of our
weariness,
shake us out of our complacency,
whisper our names once more,
and scatter your gifts of grace with wild abandon.

Break open the prisons of our inner being
and let your raging justice be our sign of liberty.

Come Holy Spirit, and lead us to places we would rather not go;
expand the horizons of our limited imaginations.
Awaken in our souls dangerous dreams for a new tomorrow,
and rekindle in our hearts the fire of prophetic enthusiasm.

Come Holy Spirit, whose justice outwits international
conspiracy;
whose light outshines spiritual bigotry,
whose peace can overcome the destructive potential of warfare,
whose promise invigorates our every effort
to create a new heaven and a new earth,
now and forever.

Diarmuid O'Murchu, O.P.

Prayer at the Western Wall

God of all the ages,
on my visit to Jerusalem, the "City of Peace,"
spiritual home to Jews, Christians, and Muslims alike,
I bring before you the joys, the hopes, and the aspirations,
the trials, the suffering, and the pain of all your people
    throughout the world.

God of Abraham, Isaac and Jacob,
hear the cry of the afflicted, the fearful, the bereft;
send your peace upon this Holy Land, upon the Middle East,
upon the entire human family;
stir the hearts of all who call upon your name,
to walk humbly in the path of justice and compassion.

"The Lord is good to those who wait for him,
to the soul that seeks him" (Lam 3:25)!
    Pope Benedict XVI

*This college will be one of the most powerful
means for doing good in this country.*
    Edward Sorin, C.S.C.
    Founder of the University of Notre Dame

Prayer for Christian Unity

Eternal God, whose image lies in the hearts of all people,
we live among peoples whose ways are different from ours,
whose faiths are foreign to us,
and whose tongues are unintelligible to us.
Help us to remember that you love all people with your great
    love,
that all religion is an attempt to respond to you,

and that the yearnings of other hearts
are much like our own and are known to you.
Help us to recognize you in the words of truth,
the things of beauty,
the actions of love about us.
We pray through Christ,
who is a stranger to no land more than another,
and to every land no less than another.
World Council of Churches

The world is torn by division—and is fixed on its differences. . . . Easing the hateful divisions between human beings is the supreme challenge of this age.
John I. Jenkins, C.S.C.
President of the University of Notre Dame

Avoiding Despair

When I despair,
I remember that all through history
the ways of truth and love have always won.
There have been tyrants and murderers,
and for a time they can seem invincible,
but in the end they always fall.
Think of it—always.
Mahatma Gandhi

Lord, Make Me Uncomfortable

God, bless me with discomfort at easy answers, half-truths, and superficial relationships, so that you will live deep in my heart.

God, bless me with anger at injustice, oppression, and exploitation of people and the earth so that I will work for justice, equity, and peace.

God, bless me with tears to shed for those who suffer so that I will reach out my hand to comfort them and change their pain with joy.

God, bless me with the foolishness to think that I can make a difference in the world, so that I will do the things which others say cannot be done.
Richard Rohr, O.F.M.

Give Me Someone

Lord,
when I am famished,
give me someone who needs food;
when I am thirsty,
give me someone who needs water;
when I am cold,
give me someone to warm;
when I am hurting,
give me someone to console;
when my cross becomes heavy,
give me another's cross to share;
when I am poor,
lead someone needy to me;
when I have no time,
give me someone to help for a moment;
when I am humiliated,
give me someone to praise;
when I am discouraged,
send someone to encourage;

when I need another's understanding,
give me someone who needs mine;
when I need somebody to take care of me,
send me someone to care for;
when I think of myself,
turn my thoughts toward another.

Vocational Prayer to Make a Difference

Lord, what good is one billion dollars
if there are three billion hungry people in the world?
Why demand *my* will when so many are denied their basic rights,
have no choices, and even live in slavery?
Why have my own children
when there are so many who are orphaned, aborted, abused,
    homeless—
who will be your light to them?

You make every vocation holy
and in all of these questions I hear you calling me to radical,
    selfless love.
You gave your priest Jacques Dujarie strength to say,
"I am a priest to be father to the orphan,
the consolation of the widow,
the support of the poor, and the friend of the suffering."
Give me strength in my discernment of a call to religious life,
that in the freeing vows of poverty, obedience, and chastity
I might be parent to the orphan, consolation of the widow,
support of the poor, and friend of the suffering.
In prayer and in ministry,
help me to bring the world your comfort and guidance,
your understanding and joy, your rest, and your peace.

Matthew Kuczora, C.S.C.

Prayer for the President

God our Father,
all earthly powers must serve you.
Help our president, [*name*],
to fulfill his/her responsibilities worthily and well.
By honoring and striving to please you at all times,
may he/she secure peace and freedom
for the people entrusted to him/her.
> ***Sacramentary***

For Those Who Serve in Public Office

Almighty and eternal God,
you know the longing of people's hearts
and you protect their rights.
In your goodness,
watch over those in authority,
so that people everywhere may enjoy
freedom, security, and peace.
> ***Sacramentary***

Prayer for World Leaders

Mother-Father God:
we ask that all our elected representatives
    and appointed officials,
as well as our business and world leaders,
be surrounded with and protected by your Light.
We ask that their every thought, word, and action
come from their Higher Selves
and serve the highest good for our country and the world.

Acknowledging our oneness with each other and with all
    creation,
we ask this in your Name.
And so it is.
    Carol Hansen Grey

A Simple Prayer

May all be fed.
May all be healed.
May all be loved.
    John Robbins

✣ ✣ ✣

10

✣ ✣ ✣

UPON
THIS ROCK

Prayers for Parish Life
and Sacramental Moments

BASILICA OF THE SACRED HEART

Every year we stand in utter darkness, hundreds of us crowded together. All light is extinguished, all hope is lost. Our Savior slain, we have heard of torment and humiliation, and then crucifixion. We stand in the darkness that has seemingly won the day. Silence, briefly, has its crippling power over us; the world waits.

As a participant in the Easter Vigil at the Basilica of the Sacred Heart on the Notre Dame campus, I've always been visually (to say nothing of faithfully) caught up in what happens on this night, the core of the paschal mystery. As the presider slowly enters the nave of the church, the pillars of the basilica stand like stubborn sentinels, lining the way down to the sanctuary. But then the single paschal candle invades this profound darkness.

It's the shadows that catch my eye, though. That solitary candle makes a shadow army of the pillars—its humble flame creates and casts their dark personalities against the walls of the church. And as the candle makes its way into the midst of the assembly, closer to the altar, deeper into the hearts of the faithful, a reverse choreography transpires: as the candle gains ground, the shadows retreat. They fall back, silently hurtling toward the door of the church, knowing they have no place with us.

Light has the last word. Shadows and darkness are removed from our sight. And from this chaotic darkness leaps the Exultet and our Easter Alleluias.

Steven C. Warner, '80 MA
Director, Notre Dame Folk Choir

THE GOSPEL
MADE PRAYER

⊹ ⊹

As a seminarian in the late 1960s, the emphasis on Mary that I had experienced growing up was fading away. After the Second Vatican Council many were now deemphasizing Mary, and most of the seminarians had put the rosary aside. I was no exception, but after ordination I was assigned to work with a Mexican American community that had a great dedication to Our Lady of Guadalupe.

In 1980 my brother Bob died at age twenty-three, leaving behind his wife and two-year-old child. The whole family was distraught, but I was somehow given the grace to be able to console them a bit and lead them in the Eucharist, praying for his eternal life. After the Mass of Resurrection and the burial, we shared stories about Bob's life and helped each other through a most difficult moment.

I returned to my work at a center in South Bend, but my heart was not in it. I could accomplish nothing. I would sit at my desk and think only of my brother and how my life, and especially the lives of his wife and child, had been changed forever. I was grieving at a level I had never anticipated.

One Mexican gentleman, observing my sadness and paralysis, suggested that I make use of the custom of his people and have a novena of rosaries said in my house to pray for my deceased brother. I accepted this idea, and was most impressed to see those I had accompanied at the time of their loss of a loved one coming to my house to kneel and pray the rosary for Bob and for me. The novena helped me greatly, and it led to my making the rosary a daily practice again. This was a powerful prayer. Meditating on

⁙

the mysteries made me realize that my brother's death was also a mystery, and that Mary, Our Lady of Guadalupe, would help my acceptance of reality the way she did with her beloved Mexicans.

The rosary had brought me back to life. I would never abandon it again. Now I promote it around the world, and I recognize its power to heal those who mourn and to unify families. Historians do not agree as to the date of the origin of the rosary, although some form of it may date back to the sixth century. In the fourteenth century, most likely, the present format was decided upon. It grew out of the desire of the laity to imitate the monks in their praying of the one hundred and fifty psalms in the Divine Office. But since most lay people could not read and had limited access to the psalms, they chose prayers they could easily memorize.

Although some think the rosary is all about Mary, it is really a Christ-centered prayer. Since Christians are to conform our lives to Christ, we refer to the rosary as a compendium of the gospel, and we use it to draw closer to our Savior.

The rosary is a wonderful way to remain close to Notre Dame, Our Lady. It is carried on one's person as a sign of the Catholic faith, though it can be used beneficially by any Christian. As the late Pope John Paul II said, it "marks the rhythm of human life." Like Father Patrick Peyton, C.S.C., the famous "Rosary Priest," the pope would pray the prayer daily, bringing to mind the mysteries of the gospel. Father Edward Sorin, C.S.C., founder of the University of Notre Dame, also had a strong Marian spirituality.

When the Mexican community came to my house to pray the rosary along with me for my deceased brother, I was moved to note that among them were members of families who had lost loved ones themselves in tragic ways. As their priest I had consoled them. Now, understanding perhaps better than myself what I was going through, they brought me consolation and peace. I could see Christ in them, comforting me in my mourning. The rosary does indeed mark the rhythm of human life. It is the gospel made prayer.

John Phalen, C.S.C.
President of Holy Cross Family Ministries

⁙

PRAYERS FOR PARISH LIFE AND SACRAMENTAL MOMENTS

✢   ✢

Do this in memory of me.
—Luke 22:19

As much as we experience God in the everyday moments of our lives, we also encounter God in a special way in our Church. The parish is where Catholics gather regularly to praise God and to seek support from others in living the Christian life. It's also where we celebrate significant milestones: new life, life-time commitments, and death. Lots of other things happen at parishes, from Bible study to bingo. But the most important event is the liturgy, where we encounter God in the Eucharist and in the People of God. At Notre Dame, the Basilica of the Sacred Heart is a parish church, but each dorm also is like a little parish, with its pajama-clad community gathering for Eucharist in the chapel. No doubt we pray *while* in church, but we also should remember to pray *for* our parishes and the priests who serve them.

Prayer for Parishes

We thank you now for this house of prayer
in which you bless your family
as we come to you on pilgrimage.

Here you reveal your presence
by sacramental signs,
and make us one with you
through the unseen bond of grace.

Here you build your temple of living stones,
and bring the Church to its full stature
as the body of Christ throughout the world,
to reach its perfection at last
in the heavenly city of Jerusalem,
which is the vision of your peace.

In communion with all the angels and saints
we bless and praise your greatness
in the temple of your glory.
Sacramentary

Prayer before Mass

Almighty and ever-living God,
I approach the sacrament
of your only-begotten Son
Our Lord Jesus Christ.

I come sick to the doctor of life,
unclean to the fountain of mercy,

blind to the radiance of eternal light,
and poor and needy to the Lord
of heaven and earth.

Lord, in your great generosity,
heal my sickness,
wash away my defilement,
enlighten my blindness, enrich my poverty,
and clothe my nakedness.

May I receive the bread of angels,
the King of kings and Lord of lords,
with humble reverence,
with the purity and faith,
the repentance and love,
and the determined purpose
that will help to bring me to salvation.
                    Adapted from St. Thomas Aquinas

Confiteor

I confess to almighty God,
and to you, my brothers and sisters,
that I have sinned through my own fault,
in my thoughts and in my words,
in what I have done, and in what I have failed to do;
and I ask blessed Mary, ever virgin,
all the angels and saints,
and you, my brothers and sisters,
to pray for me to the Lord our God.

Gloria

Glory to God in the highest,
and peace to his people on earth.

Lord God, heavenly King,
almighty God and Father,
we worship you, we give you thanks,
we praise you for your glory.

Lord Jesus Christ, only Son of the Father,
Lord God, Lamb of God,
you take away the sin of the world:
have mercy on us;
you are seated at the right hand of the Father:
receive our prayer.

For you alone are the Holy One,
you alone are the Lord,
You alone are the Most High,
Jesus Christ,
with the Holy Spirit,
in the glory of God the Father. Amen.

Nicene Creed

We believe in one God,
the Father, the Almighty
maker of heaven and earth,
of all that is seen and unseen.
We believe in one Lord, Jesus Christ,
the only Son of God,
eternally begotten of the Father,
God from God, Light from Light,

true God from true God,
begotten, not made,
one in Being with the Father.
Through him all things were made.
For us men and for our salvation
he came down from heaven:
by the power of the Holy Spirit
he was born of the Virgin Mary, and became man.

For our sake he was crucified under Pontius Pilate;
he suffered, died, and was buried.
On the third day he rose again
in fulfillment of the Scriptures;
he ascended into heaven
and is seated at the right hand of the Father.
He will come again in glory to judge the living and the dead,
and his kingdom will have no end.

We believe in the Holy Spirit, the Lord, the giver of Life,
who proceeds from the Father and the Son.
With the Father and the Son he is worshiped and glorified.
He has spoken through the Prophets.
We believe in one holy catholic and apostolic Church.
We acknowledge one baptism for the forgiveness of sins.
We look for the resurrection of the dead,
and the life of the world to come. Amen.

Prayer after Mass (*Anima Christi*)

Soul of Christ, sanctify me.
Body of Christ, save me.
Blood of Christ, inebriate me.
Water from Christ's side, wash me.
Passion of Christ, strengthen me.

⁜

O good Jesus, hear me.
Within thy wounds hide me.
Suffer me not to be separated from thee.
From the malicious enemy defend me.
In the hour of my death call me
and bid me come unto thee.
That with all thy saints
and with thy angels
I may praise thee,
forever and ever.

St. Ignatius of Loyola

Prayer for Eucharistic Adoration

In silence,
To be here before you, Lord, that's all,
to shut the eyes of my body,
to shut the eyes of my soul,
and to be still and silent,
to expose myself to you who are here,
exposed to me,
to be there before you,
the eternal presence.
I am willing to feel nothing, Lord,
to see nothing,
to hear nothing,
empty of all ideas, of all images,
in the darkness.
Here I am, simply,
to meet you without obstacles,
in the silence of faith,
before you, Lord.

Michael Quoist

✢

Apostles' Creed

I believe in God, the Father almighty, Creator of heaven and
  earth.
And in Jesus Christ, his only Son, our Lord, who was conceived
  by the Holy Spirit,
born of the Virgin Mary, suffered under Pontius Pilate,
was crucified, died, and was buried.
He descended into hell; the third day he rose again from the
  dead;
he ascended into heaven, sits at the right hand of God the Father
  almighty, from thence he shall come to judge the living and
  the dead.
I believe in the Holy Spirit, the holy Catholic Church, the
  communion of saints, the forgiveness of sins, the resurrection
  of the body, and life everlasting. Amen.

*The happiest day of my life was when I was
ordained a Catholic priest.*
Theodore M. Hesburgh, C.S.C.
President Emeritus of the University of Notre Dame

Prayer for Baptism

Lord God,
in baptism we die with Christ
to rise again in him.
Strengthen us by your Spirit
to walk in the newness of life
as your adopted children.
            Sacramentary

Prayer for Anniversary of Child's Baptism

Loving Father God, today,
as we celebrate the anniversary of our beloved child's baptism,
we recall those promises we made together
when we sought this sacrament for our child.

Please aid us in our duty to raise him/her up
to live according to your laws of love,
that he/she may always care for you
and for his/her neighbor according to your commandments.
Help us to make it our constant mission as his/her parents
to set an example of loving compassion for this child,
showing him/her through our own words and actions
our unending love for you and for one another.

As we recall today our child's anointing
as Priest, Prophet, and King,
Lord strengthen him/her in faith to worship you
as a true follower, to boldly proclaim the truth of your Word,
and to lovingly serve the poor and the afflicted in our world
with kindness and care.

Open his/her ears to receive your teachings,
and his/her mouth to proclaim his/her faith in you.

Bless his/her moments as a member of our family,
and his/her life as a part of your universal family.

May he/she know lasting happiness and grace
all the days of his/her life,
as he/she journeys ever closer to eternal life forever with you.
    Lisa Hendey, '85

Prayer for First Communion

All loving God,
you created [*name*] in your image
and gave him/her the gift of life in our family.
Through baptism you welcomed [*name*]
into your family, the church,
and called him/her to live as your son/daughter.
We thank you for this day,
on which, for the first time, [*name*] received
your Son Jesus in the Eucharist.
May we always be nourished by your presence
so as to grow in friendship with you.
As we continue our celebration around this table,
bless our food
and help us recognize Christ in one another.
We ask this in Jesus' name. Amen.
Robert M. Hamma, '83 MA

Prayer for Confirmation

Come Holy Spirit,
fill the heart of [*name*]
and kindle in him/her the fire of your love.
Send forth your Spirit, and he/she shall be created.
And you shall renew the face of the earth.

Let us pray.
O, God, who by the light of the Holy Spirit,
did instruct the hearts of the faithful,
grant that by the same Holy Spirit
[*name*] may be truly wise and ever enjoy his consolations.
Through Christ our Lord.

Prayer for a Newly Confirmed Catholic

Christ has no body but yours,
no hands, no feet on earth but yours.
Yours are the eyes with which he looks
compassion on this world.
Yours are the feet with which he walks to do good;
yours are the hands with which he blesses all the world;
yours are the hands, yours are the feet;
yours are the eyes, you are his body.
Christ has no body now but yours,
no hands, no feet on earth but yours,
yours are the eyes with which he looks
compassion on this world.
Christ has no body now on earth but yours.
      St. Teresa of Avila

Act of Contrition I

O my God, I am heartily sorry
For having offended you,
and I detest all my sins,
because I dread the loss of heaven,
and the pains of hell;
but most of all because they offend
you, my God,
who are all good and deserving of all my love.
I firmly resolve, with the help of your grace,
to confess my sins, to do penance,
and to amend my life.

Act of Contrition II

My God, I am sorry for my sins with all my heart.
In choosing to do wrong and failing to do good,
I have sinned against you whom I should love above all things.
I firmly intend, with your help, to do penance,
to sin no more, and to avoid whatever leads me to sin.
Our Savior Jesus Christ suffered and died for us.
In his name, my God, have mercy.

Prayer for Anointing of Sick

Father,
your Son, Jesus Christ, is our way, our truth, and our life.
Our brother/sister [*name*] entrusts himself/herself to you
with full confidences in all your promises.
Refresh him/her with the body and blood of your Son
and lead him/her to your kingdom in peace.
Sacramentary

Prayer for Sacrament of Marriage

Father,
you have made the bond of marriage
a holy mystery,
a symbol of Christ's love for his church.
Hear our prayers for [*name*] and [*name*].
With faith in you and in each other
they pledge their love today.
May their lives always bear witness
to the reality of that love.
Sacramentary

Prayer for a Newly Ordained Priest

Good and gracious God,
we rejoice today
in the ordination of [*name*], our brother.

We give thanks for his family
and for all those who have fostered within him
a deep love for you and for your Church.

Lord,
bestow upon [*name*] the spirit of priestly holiness.
As he baptizes in the name of the most holy Trinity,
may your people be renewed in the waters of rebirth;
as he presides at the Eucharist,
may he always be mindful of the precious gift
by which we are nourished and fed;
and as he forgives sins,
may he make present to us
the forgiving and merciful Christ.

Lord,
bless our brother with priestly zeal, compassion, and love.
As he anoints those who are sick,
may they be raised up in body and spirit;
as he joins man and woman together in marriage,
may they become a living sign of Christ's love for his Church;
and as he offers his life to those entrusted to his care,
may he follow the example of his Lord and Teacher
who came to serve, rather than be served,
Jesus Christ, your Son, who lives and reigns
for ever and ever.

      Peter Rocca, C.S.C.
      Rector, Basilica of the Sacred Heart

⊹

Prayer for Religious Profession

Lord,
you have inspired our brothers/sisters
with the resolve to follow Christ more closely.
Grant a blessed ending to the journey
on which they have set out,
so that they may be able to offer you
the perfect gift of their loving service.
> ***Sacramentary***

For Parish Ministers and Volunteers

Father,
you have taught the ministers of your Church
not to desire that they be served
but to serve their brothers and sisters.
May they be effective in their work
and persevering in their prayer,
performing their ministry
with gentleness and concern for others.
> ***Sacramentary***

Blessing of Catechists

Lord God, source of all wisdom and knowledge,
you sent your Son, Jesus Christ, to live among us
and to proclaim his message
of faith, hope, and love to all nations.

In your goodness bless our brothers and sisters
who have offered themselves as catechists for your Church.

Strengthen them with your gifts
that they may teach by word and example
the truth which comes from you.
>> **Book of Blessings**

*The prayer has great power which a
person makes with all his might.*
Mechthild of Magdeburg

Prayer for Vocations to the Priesthood and Religious Life

Lord Jesus,
as you once called the first disciples to make them fishers of men,
let your sweet invitation continue to resound: come follow me!
Give young men and women the grace of responding quickly to
    your voice.
Support our bishops, priests, and consecrated people in their
    apostolic labor.
Grant perseverance to our seminarians
and to all those who are carrying out the ideal of a life
totally consecrated to your service.
Awaken in our community a missionary eagerness.
Lord, send workers to your harvest and do not allow humanity
    to be lost
for the lack of pastors, missionaries,
and people dedicated to the cause of the Gospel.
Mary, Mother of the Church, the model of every vocation,
help us to say yes to the Lord
who calls us to cooperate in the divine plan of salvation.
>> **Pope John Paul II**

✥

Prayer for Personal Vocation

My Lord and my God,
You have formed my inmost being,
and you have made plans to give me a future full of hope.
And so I pray:
grant me the vision to perceive the gifts and talents you have
    given me,
the hearing to discern your call for me,
and above all a heart that trusts in your loving Providence.
May I follow your will for my life, which is my hope.

Grant that all people may discover and live their vocation to love
in their work in the world and amongst their families and
    friends.
Grant especially that men and women may answer the call to
    serve you
and to serve the world as vowed religious and as priests.
O God who has formed me and given me a future full of hope,
continue to form and guide me, as you form and guide all
    people.
        Michael Seidl, C.S.C.

Prayer for Our Priests

You came from among us
to be, for us, one who serves.
We thank you for ministering Christ to us
and helping us minister Christ to each other.

We are grateful for the many gifts you bring to our community:
for drawing us together in worship,
for visiting us in our homes,
for comforting us in sickness,

for showing us compassion,
for blessing our marriages,
for baptizing our children,
for confirming us in our calling,
for supporting us in bereavement,
for helping us to grow in faith,
for encouraging us to take the initiative,
for helping the whole community realize
God's presence among us.

For our part, we pray
that we may always be attentive to your needs
and never take you for granted.
You, like us, need friendship and love,
welcome and a sense of belonging,
kind words and acts of thoughtfulness.

We pray, also,
for the priests who have wounded priesthood.
May we be willing to forgive
and may they be open to healing.
Let us support one another during times of crisis.

God our Father, we ask you to bless our priests
and confirm them in their calling.
Give them the gifts they need
to respond with generosity and a joyful heart.
We offer this prayer for our priest,
who is our brother and friend.
World Day of Prayer for Priests

Prayer for Jubilee of Ordination

Loving God and Father,
you care for us and guide us always.
As we journey in this life
we have been blessed and strengthened
by the example, dedication, and service of [*name*], our brother,
who today celebrates the anniversary of his priestly ordination.
Grateful for his many years of service,
we ask that you bless and sustain him in the years ahead
that he may continue to serve you and your people
with priestly zeal, compassion, and love.
We ask this in the name of Jesus the Lord.
  Peter Rocca, C.S.C.
  Rector, Basilica of the Sacred Heart

May the God who allows and invites me to make this
commitment strengthen and protect me to be faithful to it.
From the vows taken by Holy
Cross priests and brothers

Prayer for Jubilee of Religious Vows

Almighty and eternal God,
as we walk by faith, guided by your Spirit,
we have been blessed by the life and witness
of our brother/sister, [*name*],
who today celebrates the anniversary of his/her religious
    profession
of the vows of poverty, chastity, and obedience.
Grateful for his/her many years of living the consecrated life,
we ask that you bless and strengthen him/her in the years ahead

that he/she may continue to be a true witness of Christ to all the
  world
and so draw us ever closer to you.
We make this prayer through Christ our Lord.
> **Peter Rocca, C.S.C.**
> **Rector, Basilica of the Sacred Heart**

Prayer for the Pope

God our Father, shepherd and guide,
look with love on [*name*], your servant,
the pastor of your Church.
May his word and example inspire and guide the Church,
and may he, and all those entrusted to his care,
come to the joy of everlasting life.
> ***Sacramentary***

Prayer Welcoming Returning Catholics

Lord, let me welcome all my sisters and brothers
with the arms of Christ.
May I listen to their stories
with the openness of Christ.
And may I embrace them
with the Love of Christ.
Through my hospitality,
may they once more
call our Church their home.
> **Richard Chilson, C.S.P.**

For the Church

Divine Spirit,
renew your wonders in this our age, as in a new Pentecost,
and grant that your Church,
praying perseveringly and insistently with one heart and mind
together with Mary, the Mother of Jesus,
and guided by blessed Peter,
may increase the reign of the Divine Savior,
the reign of truth and justice,
the reign of love and peace.
Pope John XXIII

✛ ✛ ✛

11

✛ ✛ ✛

PRAY
FOR US

Prayers to Mary and the Saints

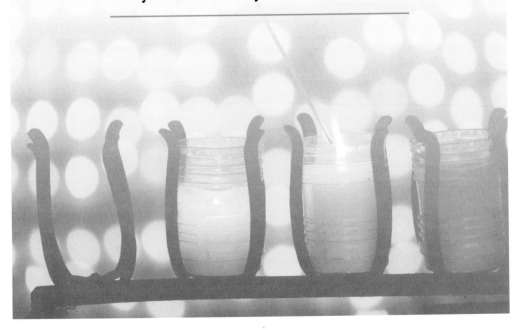

THE GOLDEN DOME

As an eager young intern at the *South Bend Tribune* in 1988, I got the plum assignment of writing about plans to regild Notre Dame's golden dome. I remember the thrill of seeing my byline on the front page of a newspaper for the first time, though, truth be told, it was a rather pedestrian piece.

I got the facts right, but missed the human interest angles: how Notre Dame founder Father Edward Sorin, C.S.C., had insisted on a golden dome and statue atop the new administration building after the previous wooden dome was destroyed by fire in 1879; how the statue of Mary, modeled after one in Rome, was paid for by donations from nuns, students, and alumnae of Saint Mary's College; how the workers from Conrad Schmitt Studios in Wisconsin had to chip off all the old gold leaf from the zinc-coated, cast-iron statue before applying the 23.9-karat, microns-thin gold leaf.

It may be Notre Dame "doctrine" that Mary resides at the Grotto, but as a student, I had trouble finding her there. Maybe there was just too much competition, what with all those candles flickering for her attention. But Mary atop the dome was always there. All I had to do was lift my eyes.

The Golden Dome is the university's most famous symbol; indeed, students and alumni refer to themselves as "domers."

Although we often like to boast, "We're #1," Mary reminds us to be humble. Even she needs a facelift every few decades.

Heidi Schlumpf, '88

OUR LADY OF ✠ GUADALUPE ✠

In one sense it is not surprising that the feast of Our Lady of Guadalupe has become a major annual event at Notre Dame's Basilica of the Sacred Heart. A growing number of Latino students, faculty, and alumni bring to the campus community their deep reverence for the Guadalupana. But what strikes us each December 12 is the number of faces in the packed basilica that are not Latino. Like many students we meet in our Latino spirituality class, most of these devotees presumably had scarcely heard of Guadalupe before they arrived at Notre Dame. Yet they join freely in the singing and the procession to the Lady Chapel after Eucharist to present her with the traditional roses that commemorate her day.

The growth of Guadalupan devotion at Notre Dame is by no means unique. Guadalupe's faithful have been expanding for nearly five centuries. Her basilica in Mexico City is the most visited pilgrimage site on the American continent. After Jesus of Nazareth, her image is the most reproduced sacred icon in the Western Hemisphere. She appears among an increasingly diverse array of peoples and places in North America and beyond: on home altars, t-shirts, tattoos, murals, parish churches, medals, refrigerator magnets, and wall hangings. Long acclaimed as the national symbol of Mexico, in the 1999 apostolic exhortation "Ecclesia in America" Pope John Paul II acclaimed her as the "mother and evangelizer of America," from Tierra del Fuego to the northernmost reaches of Canada. At the unanimous request of the Catholic bishops of the hemisphere, he also decreed that her feast "be celebrated throughout the continent."

How does Our Lady of Guadalupe attract such a rich variety of dedicated daughters and sons? What is her compelling force?

One answer is the tradition of her apparitions in 1531 to the indigenous neophyte Juan Diego, whom Pope John Paul II canonized a saint in 2002. Devotees pass on this treasured narrative to their children. They esteem the richly poetic Nahuatl language *Nican Mopohua* account, which relates how Guadalupe sent Juan Diego to request that Juan de Zumárraga, the first bishop of Mexico, build a temple in her honor on the sacred hill of Tepeyac. At first the bishop doubted the celestial origins of this request, but came to believe when Juan Diego dropped exquisite out-of-season flowers from his *tilma* (cloak) and presented the image of Guadalupe that miraculously appeared on the rough cloth of his garment. In various ways Guadalupe provided Juan Diego with hope and consolation, especially through the healing of his uncle, Juan Bernardino.

Numerous devotees resonate with the encounter between Guadalupe and Juan Diego, which they often proclaim in liturgical drama on her feast. Immigrants and others who have experienced the pain of rejection find solace in Guadalupe's election of the unexpected hero Juan Diego, and hope in Juan Diego's unwavering faith and holy *aguante* (unyielding endurance). They confess that the Guadalupe narrative is true: it reveals the deep truth of their human dignity and exposes the lie of experiences that unjustly diminish their fundamental sense of worth.

Guadalupe's faithful also contemplate her beauty, especially her compassionate face and eyes. For numerous devotees the core experience of Guadalupe is that of Juan Diego. They stand before her and relive Juan Diego's mystical encounter. Beholding their mother's countenance does not obliterate all the difficulties of daily life. But her beauty and unconditional love transform them, enabling them to confront harsh realities with the confident assurance that no human force can thwart God's loving designs.

When we assign our Notre Dame students the task of writing about their spiritual journey, invariably they recount the help of a

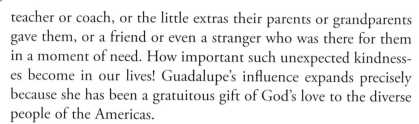

teacher or coach, or the little extras their parents or grandparents gave them, or a friend or even a stranger who was there for them in a moment of need. How important such unexpected kindnesses become in our lives! Guadalupe's influence expands precisely because she has been a gratuitous gift of God's love to the diverse people of the Americas.

Our explanations do not make Guadalupe powerful. She is powerful because she lives in the hearts and minds of people. Her loyal sons and daughters at Notre Dame enlarge the fascinating adventure initiated long ago in the eruption of God's compassion that St. Juan Diego experienced in her.

Timothy Matovina and Virgilio Elizondo
Cushwa Center for the Study of American Catholicism

PRAYERS TO MARY AND THE SAINTS

✛ ✛

Mary treasured all these words and pondered them in her heart.
—Luke 2:19

It is hard to overestimate the importance of devotion to Mary,
for Catholics in general and for the Notre Dame family in
particular. Of course, the university is named for Our Lady, and
the Grotto, modeled on the one at Lourdes, France, is probably
the most visited spot on campus. Our belief in the intercession of
Mary and all the saints is part of what defines us as Catholics. We
not only pray to God through these holy people, but their prayers
support us just as their lives inspire us.

Notre Dame, Our Mother (*Alma Mater*)

Notre Dame, Our Mother, tender strong and true,
proudly in the heavens gleams thy gold and blue,
glory's mantle cloaks thee, golden is thy fame,

and our hearts forever praise thee, Notre Dame,
and our hearts forever love thee, Notre Dame.
Charles O'Donnell, C.S.C.

Prayer at the Grotto

Dear Mother,
it is good to be here with you,
to come sit with you,
to rest in your presence
and leave all worries and anxieties in your lap.
Thank you for welcoming me with love.
Mother, my life is full with due dates, expectations,
and faces of those I love.
I come to you with a full heart,
so that you can lift me up and offer me to your Son.
I am filled with peace when I come here.
The candles, the people praying,
the trees and tolling bells
help me to clearly feel your love and prayers for me.
Please hold me close to you
and place your Son in my heart.
Catherine Bateson

Memorare

Remember, O most gracious Virgin Mary,
that never was it known
that anyone who fled to thy protection,
implored thy help, or sought thy intercession
was left unaided.
Inspired by this confidence,

I fly unto thee, O Virgin of virgins, my Mother;
to thee do I come, before thee I stand, sinful and sorrowful.
O Mother of the Word Incarnate,
despise not my petitions,
but in thy mercy, hear and answer me.
St. Bernard of Clairvaux

Prayer to Our Lady of Guadalupe

Santa María de Guadalupe,
come to us as you came to Juan Diego,
so that we might believe in ourselves as you believe in us.
Come to us as you came to Juan Bernardino,
so that we might value, celebrate, and transmit
the sacred traditions of our parents and grandparents.
Come to us as you came to Bishop Juan de Zumárraga
so that we might listen to the poor and simple of society
and hear the call of God through their cries
for recognition, understanding, and appreciation.
Let us all work together to build that temple you requested:
a space of universal welcome and fellowship
for all the peoples of this hemisphere.
Whether it is in our homes, our neighborhoods,
our cities, our nations, or the world,
let us do all we can to break down the walls of prejudice
and build up the temple of the new humanity,
a living temple of love and compassion.
Let our untiring efforts become the beautiful and alluring
    melodies
that will attract all peoples to your holy mountain
and through you to the great banquet table of our Lord Jesus
    Christ.
      Virgilio Elizondo
      Department of Theology

Beneath Your Compassion
(*Sub Tuum Praesidium*)

We turn to you for protection,
holy Mother of God.
Listen to our prayers
and help us in our needs.
Save us from every danger,
glorious and blessed Virgiin

*To that lovely Lady, raised high on a dome, a Golden
Dome, [all] may look and find the answer.*
Edward Sorin, C.S.C.
Founder of the University of Notre Dame

Prayer to Our Lady, Help of Christians

Most Holy Virgin Mary, Help of Christians,
how sweet it is to come to your feet
imploring your perpetual help.
If earthly mothers cease not to remember their children,
how can you, the most loving of all mothers, forget me?
Grant then to me, I implore you,
your perpetual help in all my necessities,
in every sorrow, and especially in all my temptations.
I ask for your unceasing help for all who are now suffering.
Help the weak, cure the sick, convert sinners.
Grant through your intercessions many vocations to the religious
    life.
Obtain for us, O Mary, Help of Christians,
that having invoked you on earth
we may love and eternally thank you in heaven.
        St. Don Bosco

A Prayer of Empathy Using the Rosary

As you hold the crucifix, say, "This is love. This (dying on the cross) is what it means to love to the highest degree. This is the Power that created and sustains the universe." As you finger the cross, think about what it really means to love someone, how you feel about those you love, how the boundary between you and the other melts away. Then think about God feeling that same way about you—and about all of creation, everywhere and for all time.

On the first "stand alone" bead, say "Let me, through my life this day be this love in the world. Let me, through my actions, answer someone's prayer today." Let me, to the best of my ability, be this word incarnate today. Each bead between the decades stands for you, in this version of the rosary.

Dedicate the individual beads of the decades to those you love. For the three beads at the beginning of the rosary, I generally think of the three people closest to me in my life, slowly putting a face on that bead in your mind's eye. Go through the decades in this way, moving from those closest to you to people you may barely know, even your enemies. Imagine seeing life through their eyes. Try to identify with them and thank God for the gift of them in your life. In between the decades, when you come to a "stand alone" bead, think of yourself and ask God to help you to become love incarnate this day.

Go full circle with a face on every bead, back to the beginning—the cross, Love, the all-powerful Primal Force, the Creator and Sustainer of the universe. None of this had to be, yet it is. You didn't have to be, yet you are. Because of Love. Think about that and be grateful, a good ending to any prayer.

John Monczunski
Notre Dame Magazine

✟ PRAYING THE ROSARY ✟

The rosary is the tradition-distilled essence of Christian devotion in which Catholics meditate on the central mysteries of Christian belief. The rosary (literally "crown of roses") began as a way for lay people to mimic monks' praying of the 150 psalms in the Liturgy of the Hours, substituting 150 Hail Marys instead. St. Dominic further popularized the practice of using beads to keep track of the prayers. More recently Father Patrick Peyton, C.S.C., known as "The Rosary Priest," spread the importance of families praying the rosary.

The rosary begins with the Apostles' Creed, an Our Father, three Hail Marys and a Glory Be, then continues with an Our Father, ten Hail Marys and a Glory Be for each "decade," or group of ten beads. With each decade there is a mystery to meditate on while praying. The three traditional groups of mysteries are the Joyful Mysteries, the Sorrowful Mysteries, and the Glorious Mysteries. To these, Pope John Paul II added the Luminous Mysteries (also called the Mysteries of Light).

The Joyful Mysteries

The Annunciation
The Visitation
The Nativity
The Presentation
The Finding of Jesus in the Temple

The Sorrowful Mysteries

The Agony in the Garden
The Scourging at the Pillar
The Crowning with Thorns
The Carrying of the Cross
The Crucifixion

The Glorious Mysteries

The Resurrection
The Ascension of Our Lord
The Descent of the Holy Spirit
The Assumption of Our Lady
The Coronation of the Blessed Virgin Mary

The Luminous Mysteries (Mysteries of Light)

The Baptism in the Jordan
The Wedding at Cana
The Proclamation of the Kingdom of God
The Transfiguration
The Institution of the Eucharist

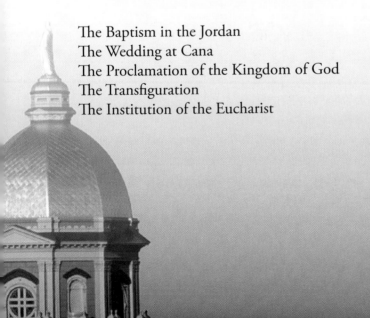

Queen of Heaven (*Regina Coeli*)

Queen of Heaven, rejoice, Alleluia,
for he whom you did merit to bear, Alleluia,
has risen, as he said, Alleluia.
Pray for us to God, Alleluia.
Rejoice and be glad, O Virgin Mary, Alleluia,
for the Lord has truly risen, Alleluia.

Let us pray.
O God, who gave joy to the world through the resurrection of
your Son, our Lord Jesus Christ, grant we beseech you, that
through the intercession of the Virgin Mary, his Mother, we may
obtain the joys of everlasting life. Through the same Christ our
Lord.

Hail, Holy Queen (*Salve Regina*)

Hail, holy Queen, Mother of mercy,
our life, our sweetness, and our hope.
To you do we cry,
poor banished children of Eve.
To you do we send up our sighs,
mourning and weeping in this vale of tears.
Turn then, most gracious advocate,
your eyes of mercy toward us,
and after this exile,
show us the blessed fruit of your womb, Jesus.
O clement, O loving,
O sweet Virgin Mary.

Angelus

Recited three times daily, at morning, noon, and evening.

The Angel of the Lord declared to Mary,
and she conceived of the Holy Spirit.
Hail Mary . . .

Behold the handmaid of the Lord.
Be it done unto me according to thy word.
Hail Mary . . .

And the Word was made Flesh
and dwelt among us.
Hail Mary . . .

Pray for us, O Holy Mother of God,
that we may be made worthy of the promises of Christ.

Let us pray.
Pour forth, we beseech thee, O Lord, thy grace into our hearts;
that we, to whom the incarnation of Christ, thy Son, was made
known by the message of an angel, may by his Passion and Cross
be brought to the glory of his Resurrection, through the same
Christ Our Lord.

Prayer to Mary

O Mary,
bright dawn of the new world,
Mother of the living,
to you do we entrust the cause of life.
Look down, O mother,
upon the vast numbers
of babies not allowed to be born,

✢

of the poor whose lives are made difficult,
of men and women who are victims of brutal violence,
of the elderly and sick killed
by indifference or out of misguided mercy.

Grant that all who believe in your Son
may proclaim the Gospel of life
with honesty and love
to the people of our time.

Obtain for them the grace
to accept that Gospel
as a gift ever new,
the joy of celebrating it with gratitude
throughout their lives
and the courage to bear witness to it
resolutely, in order to build,
together with all people of good will,
the civilization of truth and love,
to the praise and glory of God,
the Creator and lover of life.
    Pope John Paul II

St. Patrick's Breastplate

Christ with me, Christ before me,
Christ behind me, Christ in me,
Christ beneath me, Christ above me,
Christ on my right, Christ on my left,
Christ in breadth, Christ in length, Christ in height,
Christ in the heart of every person who thinks of me,
Christ in the mouth of every person who speaks of me,
Christ in every eye that sees me,
Christ in every ear that hears me.

Take, Lord, and Receive

Take, Lord, and receive
all my liberty,
my memory,
my understanding,
and my entire will—
all that I have and call my own.
You have given it all to me.
To you, Lord, I return it.
Everything is yours;
do with it what you will.
Give me only your love and your grace.
That is enough for me.
St. Ignatius of Loyola

*I rarely prayed for my mother,
but I often prayed to her.*
Blessed André Bessette, C.S.C.

Prayer of St. Thérèse of Lisieux

May today there be peace within.
May you trust God that you are exactly where you are meant to
be.
May you not forget the infinite possibilities that are born of
faith.
May you use those gifts that you have received,
and pass on the love that has been given to you.
May you be content knowing you are a child of God.

✛

Let this presence settle into your bones, and allow your soul
the freedom to sing, dance, praise, and love.
It is there for each and every one of us.

Act of Resignation

My God, I am yours for time and eternity.
Teach me to cast myself entirely
into the arms of your loving Providence
with a lively, unlimited confidence
in your compassionate, tender pity.
Grant, O most merciful Redeemer,
That whatever you ordain or permit may be acceptable to me.
Take from my heart all painful anxiety;
let nothing sadden me but sin,
nothing delight me but the hope
of coming to the possession of you,
my God and my all,
in your everlasting kingdom.
Catherine McAuley

Stay with Me

Stay with me, Jesus, for it is getting late
and the day is coming to a close,
and life passes, death, judgment, eternity approaches.
It is necessary to renew my strength,
so that I will not stop along the way
and for that, I need you.
It is getting late and death approaches.
I fear the darkness, the temptations, the dryness, the cross, the
sorrows.

O how I need you, my Jesus, in this night of exile!
Stay with me tonight, Jesus,
in life with all its dangers, I need you.

Let me recognize you as your disciples did at the breaking of
    bread,
so that the Eucharistic Communion be the light which disperses
    the darkness,
the force which sustains me, the unique joy of my heart.
Stay with me, Lord, because at the hour of my death,
I want to remain united to you,
if not by Communion, at least by grace and love.

Stay with me, Jesus, I do not ask for divine consolation,
because I do not merit it,
but, the gift of your presence, oh yes, I ask this of you!
Stay with me, Lord, for it is you alone I look for.
Your Love, your Grace, your will, your Heart, your Spirit,
I love you and ask no other reward but to love you more and
    more.
With a firm love, I will love you with all my heart while on earth
and continue to love you perfectly during all eternity.
    St. Pio of Pietrelcina (Padre Pio)

For a Holy Heart

Lord, grant me a holy heart
that sees always what is fine and pure
and is not frightened at the sight of sin,
but creates order wherever it goes.

Grant me a heart that knows nothing
of boredom, weeping and sighing.
Let me not be overly concerned with
the bothersome thing I call "myself."

Lord, give me a sense of humor
and I will find happiness in life
and profit for others.
St. Thomas More

Prayer for Guidance

O gracious and holy Father,
give us wisdom to perceive you,
intelligence to understand you,
diligence to seek you,
patience to wait for you,
eyes to see you,
a heart to meditate on you,
and a life to proclaim you,
through the power of the Spirit of Jesus Christ our Lord.
St. Benedict

Traveler's Prayer to the Angel Raphael

In the way of peace and prosperity,
may the Lord, the Almighty, direct our steps,
and may the Angel Raphael accompany us on our way,
that we may return to our home, in peace, safety, and joy.

O Lord Our God

O Lord our God,
grant us grace to desire you with a whole heart,
so that desiring you we may seek and find you;
and so finding you, may love you;

and loving you may hate those sins which separate us from you,
for the sake of Jesus Christ.
>   **St. Anselm**

Prayer of St. John of the Cross

O blessed Jesus,
give me stillness of soul in you.
Let your mighty calmness reign in me.
Rule me, O King of Gentleness,
King of Peace.

For the Canonization of Blessed Brother André, C.S.C.

Lord, you have chosen Blessed Brother André
to spread devotion to St. Joseph
and to minister to all those who are afflicted.
Through his intercession, grant us the favor that we are now
    requesting.
We also pray that the Church may canonize him as soon as
    possible.
Grant us the grace to imitate his piety and his charity
so that, with him, we may share the reward promised
to all those who care for their neighbor because of their love for
    you.

Prayer to Blessed Basile Moreau, C.S.C.

Lord Jesus,
you inspired Father Basile Moreau
to found the religious family of Holy Cross
to continue your mission among the People of God.
May he be for us a model of zealous service,
an example of fidelity,
and an inspiration as we strive to be followers of Jesus.
May the Church be moved to proclaim his saintliness
for the good of all people.
Lord Jesus, you said, "Ask and you shall receive."
I dare to come to you to ask that you hear my prayer.
It is through the intercession of Blessed Basile Moreau
that I ask [*state your intention*].
May I learn to imitate his holiness and service
and look to him confidently in times of need.

12

IT IS FINISHED

Prayers for Endings and Transitions

CEDAR GROVE
CEMETERY

When I first entered Notre Dame in 1953, I couldn't wait to get away. The draconian parietal hours—in at night by ten—made the campus feel like prison. More than once, after sneaking back out after checking in, I was chased by campus security down Notre Dame Avenue before losing them among the tombstones of Cedar Grove Cemetery.

Now the campus figures to be my eternal resting place. It took ten years of lobbying and something close to a papal dispensation to secure two plots in Cedar Grove for my wife and me, but there our bones will be. Our children are all scattered, but since they all followed us to Notre Dame and Saint Mary's College, we figured we'd be buried where we first met: that way, when the children come back for football games they can have a drink, quite literally, on us.

It's a tradition: I've often sipped a memorial martini at the grave of my beloved old professor, Frank O'Malley, who loved them.

Our final accommodations are great: there's an outdoor restroom just twenty steps away. We've a narrow view of the Basilica of the Sacred Heart away to the north, and the bookstore is two minutes by foot. We plan to erect a small stone bench—who knows, maybe in the future some of our grandchildren and great-grandchildren will find it a quiet place to study or to pray. Notre Dame, like families and graveyards, is all about communing across time and the hallowing of place.

Kenneth Woodward, '57

SAY A LITTLE PRAYER FOR ME

The German word for homesickness is *heimweh*. It was one of the first new terms I learned when I arrived in Austria in the fall of 2002 as a Notre Dame junior studying abroad for the year. It was also one of the most important. I was thousands of miles from my family, and thousands from my adopted home under the warm light of the Golden Dome. I missed them both terribly.

Austrians and Germans use *heimweh* in much the same way we use homesickness, but the meanings are slightly different. The word literally translates to "home pains," and it fit me far better than my own language's phrase. The prospect of a year apart from the people and places I loved didn't just discomfit me, it physically *hurt*.

I spent the first month of that year mired in home pains in Salzburg with the rest of the students in the program, trying to learn a new language and wishing I was just about anywhere else. My routine consisted of intensive German instruction in the mornings, followed by lunch, a good sulk, and more instruction. The late afternoons were mine and I devoted them to walking the city, alone, almost always ending up at an old monastery overlooking the town, where I would duck into a chapel and light a candle before a statue of the Blessed Mother. My prayer was a constant: that Mary would intercede for my family and friends; that the Lord, somehow, would deliver me the help and strength I needed to wriggle out of my self-pity and isolation.

Over time, God gave me what I had asked for. In October the group of students moved to Innsbruck, where we spent the academic year. I settled in, so gradually it was barely noticeable, and month by month, I did get over being hung up on my *heimweh*, though I never stopped missing everyone back home. In short, I grew. It became one of the most challenging but grace-filled times of my life; it stretched me in all the ways Notre Dame had designed the program to do. I traveled, made new friends in a language none of us had grown up speaking, and as the year drew to a close, I knew I would miss this place, too, and everyone I had met there.

In May, just before I left Austria, my mother came to visit me. The first place we traveled together was Salzburg, where I had begun all those months earlier. As we walked the city and recounted my year—the highs and the lows—my mom looked at me and smiled. "I've been praying so hard for you all this time," she said. We continued walking and eventually found ourselves climbing up toward the monastery I'd visited so many times. There, in front of us, was the chapel. It struck me that I had entirely forgotten about it. We went in, and she suggested we light a candle by Mary's statue.

At once everything came flooding back to me. And as my eyes moved back and forth between the statue of the Blessed Mother and my own mother kneeling before it, I realized that it had been her prayers (and those of everyone who cared for me) that had sustained and strengthened me, just as I had asked for so many times at that very spot. All those miles apart, it was prayer that had kept us connected through the Lord's grace and that had come to my aid. I had been completely unaware of it, but it had been there all along, all the same.

What I saw was no more and no less than that simple truth at the very heart of our faith. We are linked by prayers, like beads on a rosary, across any distance, however oblivious to them we may be in our duress. We believe in a Church that houses us at all times, in all places. It is forever in our midst. We can never be separated from it, or from those with whom we share it. We are always, always home.

Gregory Ruehlmann, '04

PRAYERS FOR ENDINGS AND TRANSITIONS

If we have died with him we shall live with him.
—2 Timothy 2:11

Just as God is present in the beginnings of our lives, so too we seek to see God's hand in the endings of life—whether in painful losses like death, or in bittersweet transitions like graduations or other leavings. Some prayers beseech God for answers, while others give thanks for God's comforting presence. Always, our prayers for endings and transitions reveal our Christian hope that death does not have the final word. In praying our goodbyes, we leave open the room for new hellos.

I Teeter on the Brink of Endings

God of endings,
you promised to be with me always,
even to the end of time.
Move with me now in these occasions of last things,
of shivering vulnerabilities and letting go:
letting go of parents gone,
past gone,
friends going,
old self growing;
letting go of children grown,
needs outgrown,
prejudices ingrown,
illusions overgrown;
letting go of swollen grudges and shrunken loves.
Be with me in my end of things,
my letting go of dead things,
dead ways,
dead words,
dead self I hold so tightly,
defend so blindly,
fear losing so frantically.
I teeter on the brink of endings:
some anticipated, some resisted,
some inevitable, some surprising,
most painful;
and the mystery of them quiets me to awe.
In silence, Lord, I feel now
the curious blend of grief and gladness in me
over the endings that the ticking and whirling of things brings;
and I listen for your leading

⊹

to help me faithfully move on through the fear
of my time to let go
so the timeless may take hold of me.
Ted Loder

Prayer for the Dead

Eternal rest grant unto him/her, O Lord,
and let perpetual light shine upon him/her;
may his/her soul and all the souls of the faithful departed,
through the mercy of God,
rest in peace.

Resurrection for us is a daily event.
**Constitution Eight
of the Congregation of Holy Cross**

Antiphons of Commendation

May the angels lead you to paradise;
may the martyrs come to welcome you
and take you to the new city,
the new and eternal Jerusalem.

May the choirs of angels welcome you.
Where Lazarus is poor no longer,
may you have eternal rest.

I am the resurrection and the life.
The man who believes in me will live,
even if he dies,
and every living person

who puts faith in me
will never suffer eternal death.
Order of Christian Funerals

Into Paradise (*In Paradisum*)

May the choirs of angels
Come to greet you.
May they lead you into paradise.
May the Lord enfold you
In his presence.
May you have eternal life.

Prayer for Those We Love

Lord God, we can hope for others nothing better
than the happiness we desire for ourselves.
Therefore, I pray you, do not separate me after death
from those I tenderly loved on earth.
Grant that where I am they may be with me,
and that I may enjoy their presence in heaven
after being so often deprived of it on earth.
Lord God, I ask you to receive your beloved children
immediately into your life-giving heart.
After this brief life on earth,
give them eternal happiness.
St. Ambrose

Psalm of Comfort

The Lord is my shepherd, I shall not want.
He makes me lie down in green pastures;
he leads me beside still waters; he restores my soul.
He leads me in right paths for his name's sake.

Even though I walk through the darkest valley,
I fear no evil; for you are with me;
your rod and your staff—they comfort me.

You prepare a table before me in the presence of my enemies;
you anoint my head with oil; my cup overflows.
Surely goodness and mercy shall follow me all the days of my life,
and I shall dwell in the house of the Lord my whole life long.
Psalm 23:1–6

Traditional Jewish Memorial Prayer

Leader: In the rising of the sun and in its going down, we remember her/him.

People: In the blowing of the wind and in the chill of winter, we remember her/him.

Leader: In the opening of buds and in the rebirth of spring, we remember her/him.

People: In the blueness of the sky and in the warmth of summer, we remember her/him.

Leader: In the rustling of leaves and in the beauty of autumn, we remember her/him.

People:	In the beginning of the year and when it ends, we remember her/him.
Leader:	When we are weary and in need of strength, we remember her/him.
People:	When we are lost and sick at heart, we remember her/him.
Leader:	When we have joys we yearn to share, we remember her/him.
All:	So long as we live, he/she too shall live, for he/she is now a part of us, as we remember her/him.

Precious Lord

Precious Lord, take my hand.
Lead me on, let me stand.
I am tired, I am weak, I am worn.
Through the storm, through the night,
lead me on to the light.
Take my hand, precious Lord,
lead me home.
Thomas Dorsey

Do Not Stand at My Grave and Weep

Do not stand at my grave and weep,
I am not there, I do not sleep.
I am in a thousand winds that blow,
I am the softly falling snow.
I am the gentle showers of rain,

⸖

I am the fields of ripening grain.
I am in the morning hush,
I am in the graceful rush
of beautiful birds in circling flight.
I am the starshine of the night.
I am in the flowers that bloom,
I am in a quiet room.
I am in the birds that sing,
I am in each lovely thing.
Do not stand at my grave and cry,
I am not there. I do not die.
Mary Elizabeth Frye

Prayer after Miscarriage or Stillbirth

God, we are weary and grieved.
We were anticipating the birth of a child,
but the promise of life was ended too soon.
Our arms yearned to cradle new life,
our mouths to sing soft lullabies.
Our hearts ache from the emptiness and the silence.
We are saddened and we are angry.
We weep and we mourn.
Weep with us, God, Creator of Life,
for the life that could not be.
Source of healing, help us to find healing
among those who care for us
and those for whom we care.
Shelter us under wings of love
and help us to stand up again for life
even as we mourn our loss.
Sandy Eisenberg Sasso

Menopause Prayer

God, source of all understanding,
be with me as the changes happen in my body.
Help me to remember that
it is a normal process for every woman.

Help me to come to terms with my changing moods.
Take away my feelings of guilt when my temper frays.
Make me seek medical advice if this is needed.

May this be a time of new assessment,
a time to look at new horizons,
at new opportunities,
and may I never lose sight of my part
in your creation.
Rosemary Atkins

*In the presence of death, religion
gives hope and strength.*
William Corby, C.S.C.
Former president of the University of Notre Dame
and chaplain at the Battle of Gettysburg

Getting Older

Jesus, who never grew old,
it is not easy for any of us to face old age.
It is fine to be young, attractive, strong.
Old age reminds us of weakness and dependence on others.
But to be your disciple means accepting weakness and
interdependence.
Because of you we can rejoice in weakness in ourselves,

⁜

and be tender to it in others.
Monica Furlong

Prayer for Midlife

To be fully human, fully myself,
to accept all that I am, all that you envision,
this is my prayer.
Walk with me out to the rim of life,
beyond security.
Take me to the exquisite edge of courage
and release me to become.
Sue Monk Kidd

Hail the Cross, Our Only Hope.
Motto of the Congregation of Holy Cross

Blessing for Transition

May the blessing of light be on you,
light without and light within.
May the blessed sunlight shine upon you
and warm your heart till it glows
like a great peat fire, so that the stranger may come
and warm himself at it, as well as the friend.
And may the light shine out of the eyes of you,
like a candle set in the windows of a house,
bidding the wanderer to come in out of the storm.

And may the blessing of the rain be on you—the soft sweet rain.
May it fall upon your spirit
so that all the little flowers may spring up,

and shed their sweetness on the air.
And may the blessing of the great rains be on you,
that they beat upon your spirit and wash it fair and clean,
and leave there many a shining pool, and sometimes a star.

And may the blessing of the earth be on you—the great round
    earth;
May you ever have a kindly greeting for people you pass
as you are going along the roads.
    Traditional Irish Blessing

Prayer for Aging Parents

Lord, watch over our aging parents.
Keep them healthy, active, and ever growing closer to you.
Should their increasing years bring them
isolation, distress, or weakness,
assure them of your faithfulness.
Comfort them with the knowledge that their lives were well
    spent.
Enable our parents to serve you well
through their remaining time on earth.
Help them to appreciate their many blessings.
Encourage them to face death with peace, not fear.
Remind them that old age comes from you and leads to you.
Jesus, we commit to your care our parents' final years.
    Kathleen M. Sullivan, '82 MA, '87 PhD

Do Not Fear Change

Do not look forward in fear to the changes in life.
Rather, look to them with full hope that as they arise,

God, whose very own you are,
will lead you safely through all things;
and when you cannot stand it,
God will carry you in his arms.
Do not fear what may happen tomorrow.
The same understanding Father who cares for you today
will take care of you then and every day.
He will either shield you from suffering
or will give you unfailing strength to bear it.
Be at peace, and put aside all anxious thoughts and imaginations.
    St. Francis de Sales

Prayer for Discernment III

Lord I know that you love me and that you have great plans for
    me.
But sometimes I am overwhelmed by the thought of my future.
Show me how to walk forward one day at a time.
As I explore the various options which lie before me,
help me to listen openly to others, and to pay attention
to what is in the depth of my own heart.
In this way, may I hear your call to a way of life
which will allow me to love as only I can,
and allow me to serve others
with the special gifts you have given me.
    Dominican Sisters of Grand Rapids, Michigan

Prayer to Do God's Will

My Lord God,
I have no idea where I am going.
I do not see the road ahead of me

nor do I really know myself,
and the fact that I think I am following your will
does not mean that I am actually doing so.
But I believe that the desire to please you
does in fact please you.
And I hope that I will never do anything
apart from that desire.
And I know that if I do this,
you will lead me by the right road
though I may know nothing about it.
Therefore will I trust you always though
I may seem to be lost and in the shadow of death.
I will not fear, for you are ever with me,
and you will never leave me
to face my struggles alone.
      Thomas Merton

Parents' Prayer for a Child Going to College

Loving God,
Be present with us during this time of transition,
a time of letting go, a time for spreading wings.
Send down your blessing upon our child beginning college.
Let there be loving friendships, new challenges, and rich
    opportunities
to grow in wisdom, age, and grace.
Be a source of strength and support, guidance and protection.

Send down your blessing upon us as parents.
Help us to live with the anxiety that comes with letting go
and to trust in your divine plan.
Let there be pride and joy in future accomplishments,
a deepening commitment to all you call us to as parents,

and patient love and support from afar until we celebrate the
homecomings.
Be our source of strength and support, guidance and protection.

Sylvia and John Dillon
Campus Ministry

For Child Leaving Home

God be with you in every pass,
Jesus be with you on every hill,
Spirit be with you on every stream,
headland and ridge and lawn;
each sea and land, each moor and meadow,
each lying down, each rising up,
in the trough of the waves, on the crest of the billows,
each step of the journey you go.

Traditional Irish Blessing

Graduate's Prayer

Father, I have knowledge,
so I pray you'll show me now how to use it wisely
and find a way somehow
to make the world I live in a little better place,
and make life with its problems a bit easier to face.
Grant me faith and courage and put purpose in my days,
and show me how to serve you in the most effective ways—
so all my education, my knowledge, and my skill
may find their true fulfillment as I learn to do your will.

And may I ever be aware in everything I do
that knowledge comes from learning and wisdom comes from
  you.
  St. Peter, Prince of the Apostles Catholic Church
  Corpus Christi, Texas

For Notre Dame Graduation

May the Golden Dome of Notre Dame shine upon you.
May the special sons and daughters of Notre Dame be forever.
May the spirit of Notre Dame bring you everlasting joy.
May the fires of Our Lady's Grotto
always burn brightly in your life.
And may God, Country, and Notre Dame
be a beacon on your journey.
  Rick Childress

Blessing for Graduate Students

Lord God,

In the midst of this honor ceremony, we thank you for all the talents and energies and perseverance that fill these graduate students. Their fine minds and hearts and bodies have accomplished amazing academic goals. As they step into the future, we ask your blessing on each one as they go forward into their respective professions.

May they treasure the best of the past as they accept the challenge of taking new steps into an unfolding future filled with people who will hope in them and depend on them.

May they exercise moral leadership in very daily ways as they face demanding responsibilities and decisions.

May they contribute in whatever way they can to the good life of all peoples—those close by and those in faraway places.

Lord God bless these accomplished women and men as they grow into fine leaders and mentors. May all their professional service—all their teaching, research, and learning—fill them with the gift of wisdom that is grace-filled and long lasting.

Finally, we ask your blessing on the families and friends and on all the professors and mentors and staff that have brought these graduates to this moment of celebration.

Jean Lenz, O.S.F.
Office of Student Affairs (retired)

A Prayer for Someone in Transition

Lord Jesus, your life, death, and resurrection reveal to us the face of God and teach us how to live the every day and the special days. Thank you for your lessons of dying and rising that teach us how to live. Lord, right now I am between ending and beginning, living an in-between moment. Thank you for what has been, for the people, the days shared, and the good memories. Help me to trust you, Lord, and to believe that the road ahead will give you glory. At this moment I do not see that road clearly. Give me confidence to trust your spirit as I walk into a new day.

Mary Louise Gude, C.S.C.
Division for Mission, Saint Mary's College

Prayer of One Who Is Moving On

Guardian, Guide, no pillar of cloud by day nor fire by night,
yet I sense your presence with me, God of the journey.
You are walking with me into a new land.
You are guarding me in my vulnerable moment.
You are dwelling within me as I depart from here.
You are promising to be my peace as I face the struggles
of distance from friends and security,
the planting of feet and heart in a strange place.

Renew in me a deep trust in you. Calm my anxiousness.
As I reflect on my life I can clearly see
how you have been there in all of my leavings,
You have been there in all of my comings.
You will always be with me in everything.
I do not know how I am being resettled,
but I place my life into the welcoming arms of your love.

Encircle my heart with your peace.
May your powerful presence run like a strong thread
through the fibers of my being.
  Joyce Rupp

Prayer of One Experiencing Divorce

Father, I belong to you.
I place myself anew in your hands
and acknowledge you as Master and Lord of my life.
Grant me the gift of a forgiving heart
and cleanse me of any anger, hostility, or revenge.
Heal my hurts and teach me to rely on your love.
Grant me wisdom of heart
and strengthen me by your grace to move on

in faith, in trust, and in love.
Thank you, Lord, for your love in my life.
Catholic Doors Ministry

Prayer for Those Experiencing Divorce

Dear God,
Those who show pity but forget compassion,
        I forgive.
Those who feel I have sinned,
    I am weak, or I am at fault,
        I forgive.
Those who pull away from me—
    whether from their own confusion,
    their own embarrassment,
    their own sense of marital vulnerability,
    or their inability to speak to my pain,
        I forgive.
Those who label me unlovable,
        I forgive.
Those who see me as "too available"
    and assume I will participate in immoral behavior,
        I forgive.
Those who reach out to the widowed
    with casseroles,
    inclusion in social activities,
    and deep expressions of sorrow—
        but forget my presence
        in that same lonely and confused community,
        I forgive.
Those who make me the object of their gossip
    as they explore and distort my life story,
        I forgive.

The Church
   who sees me as neither married, single, nor divorced,
   who sees me as some faceless half couple,
   who labels me as a "failed marriage participant,"
   who finds the need to annul that which was
      once very dear to me,
         I forgive.
Society, as it labels my family "broken,"
         I forgive.
Friends who have left me for whatever reasons,
         I forgive.
Parents and children,
   who are embarrassed and ashamed of my singleness
     and life choices,
         I forgive.
My absent spouse,
      to whom I am still tied by confusing emotions,
   who left me with a mixture of
     good and bad experiences and memories,
   who wounded and harmed me in very deep ways,
         I forgive.
Myself
   And whatever sense of personal failure
     I have appropriated,
         for my shortcomings,
         my very real humanity,
         my lapses into despair,
         my self-pity journeys,
         my unbridled anger,
         my discovery of jealousy, envy,
  and other undesirable character traits,
     my desire to cling
         to unhealthy but familiar life patterns
         instead of looking with hope and trust to you,
         I forgive.
      Vicki Wells Bedard and William E. Rabior

⊹

Prayer for Leaving Home

O God, you led your servant Abraham from his home
and guarded him in all his wanderings.
Guide this servant of yours, [*name*].
Be a refuge on the journey, shade in the heat,
shelter in the storm, rest in weariness,
protection in trouble, and a strong staff in danger.
For all our days together, we give thanks:
bind us together now, even though we may be far apart.
Catholic Household Blessings and Prayers

No prayer is ever lost.
St. John Vianney

Prayer for One Leaving on a Journey

May the road rise up to meet you.
May the wind be always at your back.
May the sun shine warm upon your face;
the rains fall soft upon your fields,
and until we meet again,
may God hold you in the palm of his hand.
Traditional Irish Blessing

Prayer for the Death of a Pet

Dear Lord,
Today I dwell in sadness because my beloved pet has died.
This creature was a special part of my life and cannot be replaced.
She was my loyal companion and steadfast supporter.

She loved me without bound and without condition,
and in her eyes my imperfections vanished.
In turn, I could love her without reservation or fear.

Of course there were days when she tried my patience,
when she messed up my floors or ruined my possessions.
There were days when caring for her seemed a burden.

But these could never outweigh my gratitude
for the loving companionship she gave me.
When I was lonely, she playfully reminded me I was not really
    alone.
When I was sad, she snuggled close and comforted me,
breathing new life back into me.

I watched her move through her years
and marveled at God's creation of this intricate beast.
And I stood in surprise at her cleverness,
revealing depths of spirit I could not have imagined.
She reminded me that I, too, am a creature of God,
not a creator and controller, as I often like to think.

Lord, there is now an empty space in my home,
and an uneasy silence when I return home
and do not find her there to welcome me.
Please help me to find peace in this loss,
to reflect on the happy memories we made together.

I don't know if pets go to heaven, or if we shall meet again,
but I take comfort in your infinite wisdom
and know that my pet is in the care of her creator.
May her memory live long and precious in my mind.
    Tara Dix Osborne, '98

Farewell Blessing I

May the long time sun
shine upon you,
all love surround you,
and the pure light within you
guide your way on.
Traditional Yoga Blessing

Farewell Blessing II

May the Lord bless you and keep you.
May he show his face to you and have mercy.
May he turn his countenance to you and give you peace.
The Lord bless you!
Numbers 6:24–26

Irish Farewell Blessing

Deep peace of the running wave to you.
Deep peace of the flowing air to you.
Deep peace of the quiet earth to you.
Deep peace of the shining stars to you.
Deep peace of the shades of night to you.
Moon and stars always giving light to you.
Deep peace of the infinite peace to you.

Final Blessing

I leave you now with this prayer:
that the Lord Jesus will reveal himself to each one of you,
that he will give you the strength to go out
and profess that you are Christian,
that he will show you that he alone can fill your hearts.
Accept his freedom and embrace his truth,
and be messengers of the certainty that you have been truly
    liberated
through the death and resurrection of the Lord Jesus.
This will be the new experience, the powerful experience,
that will generate, through you, a more just society and a better
    world.
God bless you, and may the joy of Jesus be always with you.
    Pope John Paul II

✜ AFTERWORD ✜

Carrying the Notre Dame Spirit into the World

The spirit of Notre Dame is elusive. My predecessor, Father Edward Malloy, put it well when he said that the university president's job is to convey this spirit—even though experiencing it is more powerful than talking about a feeling "constituted by no one aspect of the institution in isolation, but by a whole range of values, traditions, and practices seen in concert." His predecessor, Father Theodore Hesburgh, said the Notre Dame spirit is easier to describe than to define.

Aware then that an exhaustive definition is impossible, I have noted that two themes come up often in descriptions of the Notre Dame spirit: community and purpose. The two are related because the community that is created here gathers to pursue a single purpose. We aim to achieve Father Edward Sorin's mission of being "one of the most powerful means of doing good in this country" through education and inquiry in the context of faith. The collective struggle toward the same goal forges a sense of shared experience that makes community meaningful.

Still, the exact manifestation of this spirit is often unique to each individual. It can be felt for some in a quiet moment with Our Lady at the Grotto or in the solidarity of swaying to the alma mater with linked arms. Others feel it walking the hall of a campus dorm, where wide-open doors welcome friendships that will last a lifetime. Others mention a teacher who opened invisible doors in the mind. Some find it in the outpouring of community service the students give during their time here and after they leave. Some talk about the unexpected excitement the first sight of the Golden Dome stirs after an extended time away.

Away from a supportive community, identifying and living out the mission can be more challenging. Normal days may involve vying with a colleague for a promotion, or finding the energy to offer extra help to a student outside of class. An opportunity to increase profits by cutting a few corners may tempt a struggling small business owner. A teenage son or daughter may try one's patience, or a marriage may require extra attention to make it work. Yet the spirit may be manifest in these struggles, too, and often it is through prayer that we are able to reconnect with a sense of purpose in our daily lives.

The spirit of Notre Dame must not exist solely for the sake of having good times and pleasant memories. Nor should it exist solely for the sake of preserving and promoting this wonderful institution. We need to shine our light as brightly as possible, aiming it intentionally into the darkest recesses of hopelessness. We need to grow beyond the comfort of our community. We need to cultivate the gifts that this spirit of Notre Dame gives us, and we need to treasure and celebrate the fruits. After all, the gospel says that we shall be known and judged by our fruits. Notre Dame graduates have always been and will always be the most persuasive means for carrying forth the spirit of Notre Dame into the world.

We should approach the Notre Dame spirit with a desire to share rather than accumulate. If it is hoarded like a scarce commodity, it withers on the vine. But when it is given freely, it blooms into fruit. My sincere hope is that this book of essays and prayers helps you capture the Notre Dame spirit, but also inspires you to spread it throughout the world.

John I. Jenkins, C.S.C.
President of the University of Notre Dame

✢ ACKNOWLEDGMENTS ✢

Every effort has been made to properly acknowledge the sources of the prayers contained herein. When authorship is unknown, no attribution has been stated. Please inform the publisher of any omissions or amendments to these acknowledgments. Corrections will be made upon the next printing.

Thanks to the following members of Holy Cross who submitted prayer suggestions: John M. DeRiso, C.S.C., William Dygert, C.S.C., Bill Faiella, C.S.C., James Gallagher, C.S.C., Tony Grasso, C.S.C., and Elizabeth Panero, C.S.C.

1. IN THE BEGINNING

"Beginning to Pray" is reprinted from *Signs of Grace: Meditations on the Notre Dame Campus*, copyright © 2007 by Nicholas Ayo, C.S.C. Used by permission of Rowman and Littlefield Publishers, Inc.

"I Tremble on the Edge of a Maybe" is reprinted from *Guerrillas of Grace*, copyright © 1984, 2005 by Ted Loder. Used by permission of Augsburg Books.

"Prayer for the First Day of the Year" is used by permission of St. Peter, Prince of the Apostles Catholic Church, Corpus Christi, Texas, www .stpeterprince.net.

"New Year's Prayer for World Day of Peace" is from a homily of Pope John Paul II, January 1, 2003.

"Epiphany House Blessing" is reprinted from *Book of Blessings*, copyright © 1987 by the International Commission on English in the Liturgy, Inc. Used by permission.

"Prayer for Those Adopting a Child" is from *Prayers of Our Hearts in Word and Action*, copyright © 1991 by Vienna Cobb Anderson.

"Prayers for a New Grandchild" is reprinted from *Prayers for the Later Years*, copyright © 1972 by Josephine Robertson.

"Blessing of a New Pet" is reprinted from *Blessings for God's People: A Book of Blessings for All Occasions*, copyright © 1995 by Rev. Thomas G. Simons. Used by permission of Rev. Thomas G. Simons.

"Prayer for a New Attitude" is reprinted from *Markings*, copyright © 1964 by Dag Hammarskjöld.

2. OF THE HOURS

"Simple Morning Prayer" by St. Clare is reprinted from *St. Clare Prayer Book*, copyright © 2008 by Jon M. Sweeney.

"Teach My Heart Today" is reprinted from *Sacred Poems and Prayers of Love*, copyright © 1998 by Mary Ford-Grabowsky.

"Morning Offering" is reprinted from the website of The Apostleship of Prayer, www.apostleshipofprayer.org.

The English translations of the "*Benedictus*," "*Magnificat*," and "*Nunc Dimittis*" are by The International Consultation on English Texts.

"Noon Prayer" and "Night Prayer" are reprinted from *The Liturgy of the Hours*, copyright © 1970, 1973, 1975 by the International Commission on English in the Liturgy, Inc. Used by permission.

"Evening Prayer I" is reprinted from *Letters and Papers from Prison* by Dietrich Bonhoeffer, translation copyright © 1953, 1967, 1971 by SCM Press Ltd.

"O Radiant Light" copyright © 1979 by William G. Storey.

"Child's Evening Prayer" is reprinted from *The Bam Bam Clock*, copyright © 1920 by J.P. McEvoy.

"During a Sleepless Night" is reprinted from *In Times of Illness: Prayers of Hope and Strength*, copyright © 2004 by Robert M. Hamma. Used by permission of Ave Maria Press.

3. BLESS US, O LORD

"Father, Son, Spirit, Holy" is reprinted from *Leaping: Revelations & Epiphanies*, copyright © 2003 by Brian Doyle. Used by permission.

"Children's Grace" is reprinted from *Simple Prayers of Love and Delight*, copyright © 2001 by Lois Rock.

"Irish Grace" is from an anonymous booklet titled *Graces with a Celtic Flavor*.

"Bread Blessing" is reprinted from *Book of Blessings*, copyright © 1987 by the International Commission on English in the Liturgy, Inc. Used by permission.

"Remembering the Hungry" is reprinted from the website of the Huron Hunger Fund, www.diohuron.org/parishes_ministries/HHF/huron hungerfund.htm

"Birthday Blessing for an Adult" and "Birthday Blessing for a Child" are reprinted from *A Prayer Book for Catholic Families*, copyright © 2008 by Christopher Anderson. Used by permission of Loyola Press.

"Searching for a Life Partner" is reprinted from *Lead, Kindly Light*, copyright © 2005 by the University of Notre Dame Campus Ministry. Used by permission.

"Prayer for Loved Ones" is reprinted from *Friendship and Community*, copyright © 2000 by Cistercian Publications. Published by Liturgical Press, Collegeville, MN. Reprinted with permission.

"Parenting Prayer" by Renee Miller is reprinted from the website explorefaith .org, copyright © 1999–2010 explorefaith.org. Used by permission.

"Blessing of Children" is reprinted from *Book of Blessings*, copyright © 1987 by the International Commission on English in the Liturgy, Inc. Used by permission.

"Prayer on a Wedding Anniversary" is reprinted from *The Abbey Prayer Book*, by M. Basil Pennington, copyright © 2002 by Ligouri Publications, www.ligouri.org. Used by permission.

"Prayer for Mother's Day," copyright © 2009 by Jill Ann Terwilliger, whatlove canaccomplish.blogspot.com. Used by permission.

"Prayer for Father's Day" by Kirk Loadman-Copeland is reprinted from www .firstuniversalist.org. Used by permission.

"Prayer for Military Families" is reprinted from *Armed with the Faith*, Catholic Information Service, The Knights of Columbus.

"Prayer for Family Reunion" is reprinted from *Catholic Household Blessings and Prayers*, copyright © 1988 by the United States Catholic Conference. Used by permission of USCCB Publishing.

4. GLORY AND PRAISE TO OUR GOD

The English translation of "*Te Deum*" is by the International Consultation on English Texts.

"Praise to the Trinity" is reprinted from *Symphonia*, copyright © 1998 by Barbara Newman (translator). Used by permission of Cornell University Press.

5. WORK OF HUMAN HANDS

"Lord of All Hopefulness" by Jan Struther is reprinted from *Songs of Praise*, Oxford University Press, 1931. Used by permission.

"Boss's Prayer" is reprinted from *All Desires Known*, copyright © 2006 by Janet Morley. Used by permission of Morehouse Publishing.

"For Conflict with a Coworker or Friend" by Pam Weaver is excerpted from *Women of Prayer*, copyright © 1999 by Dorothy Stewart.

"Prayer for Meetings" is reprinted from the Benedictine Health System, www .bhshealth.org. Used by permission.

"Prayer for Scientists" is reprinted from *Arrowsmith*, copyright © 1925 by Sinclair Lewis.

Prayers for the Army, Navy, Marine Corps, Air Force, and Coast Guard are reprinted from *Armed with the Faith*, Catholic Information Service, The Knights of Columbus.

"Prayer for Students" is reprinted from *Day by Day: The Notre Dame Prayer Book for Students*, copyright © 1975, 2004 by Ave Maria Press. Used by permission.

"A Child's Summer Vacation Prayer" is reprinted from *Kids Book of Everyday Prayers*, copyright © 2002 by Catherine Odell. Used by permission of Loyola Press.

6. LORD, HEAR OUR PRAYER

"We Did Not Want It Easy, God" by Anna McKenzie is excerpted from *Laughter, Silence and Shouting*, copyright © 1994 by Kathy Keay.

"To the Great Questioner" is reprinted from *Seasons of Your Heart*, copyright © 1991 by Macrina Wiederkehr. Used by permission of HarperCollins Publishing.

"Prayer after Suicide" (abridged) is reprinted from *Arise from Darkness*, copyright © 1995 by Benedict Groeschel. Used by permission of Ignatius Press.

"For Those with Cancer" is reprinted from *Prayers of Our Hearts in Word and Action*, copyright © 1991 by Vienna Cobb Anderson.

"Blessing for Cancer Treatment" is reprinted from *Seasons of Survival* by Diann L. Neu. Used by permission of the Women's Alliance for Theology, Ethics and Ritual (WATER), 8121 Georgia Ave., Suite 310, Silver Spring, MD 20910, dneu@hers.com.

"Prayer for Natural Disaster" is reprinted from World Day of Prayer 2007, www.wdpusa.org, copyright © 2007 World Day of Prayer USA Committee. Used by permission.

"Blessing (*Beannacht*)" is reprinted from *Anam Cara*, copyright © 1998 by John O'Donohue. Used by permission of HarperCollins.

"Feeling Hope after Suffering" is reprinted from *Psalms of a Laywoman*, copyright © 1999 by Edwina Gateley. Used by permission of Sheed & Ward.

7. NOW THANK WE ALL OUR GOD

"Absolution" is reprinted from *New Zealand Prayer Book*, copyright © 1989 by The Anglican Church in Aotearoa, New Zealand and Polynesia.

"Gratitude for Family" and "Gratitude for Friends" are reprinted from the website explorefaith.org, copyright © 1999–2010 explorefaith.org. Used by permission.

"Gratitude for Small Things" is reprinted from *Prayers of Our Hearts in Word and Action*, copyright © 1991 by Vienna Cobb Anderson.

8. TO EVERYTHING THERE IS A SEASON

"Fall Prayer" is reprinted from *Journal of a Solitude*, copyright © 1973 by May Sarton. Used with permission of Norton.

"Prayer for Autumn Days" is reprinted from *May I Have This Dance?*, copyright © 1992 by Joyce Rupp. Used by permission of Ave Maria Press.

"A Prayer in Winter" and "A Prayer for Rain" are reprinted by permission of the National Catholic Rural Life Conference, www.ncrlc.com.

"In Praise of Summer" by Hildegard of Bingen is reprinted from *Meditations with Hildegard of Bingen*, copyright © 1982 by Bear & Co.

"Light and Darkness" by Mark Neilsen is reprinted from *The Lord is Near*, copyright © 1993 by Creative Communications for the Parish. Used by permission of the author.

"Christmas Prayer" is reprinted from *Soul Weavings*, edited by Lyn Klug, Augsburg, 1996.

"Lenten Psalm of Longing" is reprinted from *Prayers for a Planetary Pilgrim*, copyright © 1989, 2008 by Edward M. Hays. Used by permission of Ave Maria Press.

"Good Friday Prayer before a Crucifix," written in 1937 by Caryll Houselander, is reprinted from *Caryll Houselander: Essential Writings*, copyright © 2005 by Orbis Books.

"Prayer for Holy Saturday" is reprinted from *Holy Lent*, copyright © 1975 by Liturgical Press.

"Easter Vigil" is from a homily of Pope John Paul II, March 30, 2002.

"Easter Prayer" is reprinted from *Bread of Tomorrow*, copyright © 1992 by Christian Aid.

"Ascension Prayer" is reprinted from *Prayers for Dawn and Dusk*, copyright © 1992 by Edward F. Gabriele.

9. THY KINGDOM COME

"Prayer for Social Justice" is reprinted from *WomanPrayerWomanSong: Resources for Ritual*, copyright © 1987 by Medical Mission Sisters. Used by permission.

"To Love Your Enemies" is excerpted from a speech titled "Love Your Enemies" by Martin Luther King Jr. on November 17, 1957. Reprinted from www.mlkonline.net.

"That None Should Be Lost," "Prayer for the President," and "For Those Who Serve in Public Office" are reprinted from *Sacramentary*, copyright © 1973 by the International Commission on English in the Liturgy, Inc.

"Prayer for the Homeless" is reprinted from *Prayers of Our Hearts in Word and Action*, copyright © 1991 by Vienna Cobb Anderson.

"Prayer of the Farm Workers' Struggle" is reprinted from the website of the Cesar E. Chavez Foundation, www.cesarechavezfoundation.org. Used by permission.

"Give Me Someone," Anonymous, Japan, twentieth century, adapted from a translation by Mary Theresa McCarthy, in *WomanPrayers*, copyright © 2003 by Mary Ford-Grabowsky.

"Prayer at the Western Wall" by Pope Benedict XVI, Jerusalem, May 12, 2009, copyright © 2009, Libreria Editrice Vaticana.

"A Simple Prayer" is reprinted from *The Food Revolution*, www.foodrevolution.org.

10. UPON THIS ROCK

"Prayer for Parishes," "*Confiteor*," "*Gloria*," "Nicene Creed," "Prayer for Baptism," "Prayer for Anointing of Sick," "Prayer for Sacrament of Marriage," "Prayer for Religious Profession," "Prayer for Parish Ministers and Volunteers," and "Prayer for the Pope" are reprinted from *Sacramentary*, copyright © 1973 by the International Commission on English in the Liturgy, Inc.

"Prayer for Eucharistic Adoration" is reprinted from *Prayers*, copyright © 1963 by Michael Quoist. Used by permission of Sheed & Ward.

"Act of Contrition II" is reprinted from *The Rite of Penance*, copyright © 1974 by the International Commission on English in the Liturgy, Inc. Used by permission.

"Prayer for First Communion" by Robert M. Hamma is reprinted from *Let's Say Grace*, copyright © 1995 by Ave Maria Press. Used by permission of the author.

"Blessing of Catechists" is reprinted from *Book of Blessings*, copyright © 1987 by the International Commission on English in the Liturgy, Inc. Used by permission.

"Prayer Welcoming Returning Catholics" ("Landings Prayer") is reprinted from *Prayers for the Road Home*, copyright © 2001 by The Missionary Society of St. Paul in New York State. Used by permission of Paulist Press.

11. PRAY FOR US

"Prayer at the Grotto" by Catherine Bateson is reprinted from *Lead, Kindly Light*, copyright © 2005 by the University of Notre Dame Campus Ministry. Used by permission.

"Prayer to Our Lady of Guadalupe" is reprinted from *The Treasure of Guadalupe*, copyright © 2006 by Virgilio Elizondo. Used by permission of Rowman and Littlefield Publishers, Inc.

"Prayer to Mary" by Pope John Paul II is reprinted from the encyclical *The Gospel of Life*, copyright © 1995.

"Prayer to Blessed Basile Moreau" is reprinted from the University of Notre Dame website: http://moreau.nd.edu.

12. IT IS FINISHED

"I Teeter on the Brink of Endings" is reprinted from *Guerrillas of Grace*, copyright © 1984, 2005 by Ted Loder. Used by permission of Augsburg Books.

"Antiphons of Commendation" are reprinted from the *Order of Christian Funerals*, copyright © 1973 by the International Commission on English in the Liturgy, Inc.

"Precious Lord," copyright © 1938 by Hill & Range Songs, Inc. Copyright renewed, assigned to Unichappell Music, Inc. (Rightsong Music, Publisher). Used by permission of Hal Leonard Corporation.

"Prayer after Miscarriage or Stillbirth" is reprinted from *Jewish Women on Life Passages and Personal Milestones, Vol. 1*, copyright © 1994 by Sandy Eisenberg Sasso. Used by permission of Jewish Lights Publishing.

"Menopause Prayer" is reprinted from *Joined in Love*, copyright © 1988 by Rosemary Atkins.

"Getting Older" is reprinted from *Soul Weavings*, edited by Lyn Klug, Augsburg, 1996.

"Prayer for Midlife" is reprinted from *When the Heart Waits*, copyright © 1990 by Sue Monk Kidd. Used by permission of HarperCollins.

"Prayer to Do God's Will" is reprinted from *Thoughts in Solitude*, copyright © 1956, 1958 by The Abbey of Our Lady of Gethsemani.

"Graduate's Prayer" is used by permission of St. Peter, Prince of the Apostles Catholic Church, Corpus Christi, Texas. stpeterprince.net.

"For Notre Dame Graduation" by Rick Childress, father of a Notre Dame grad, is reprinted from *Lead, Kindly Light*, copyright © 2005 by the University of Notre Dame Campus Ministry. Used by permission.

"Prayer of One Who Is Moving On" is reprinted from *Praying Our Goodbyes*, copyright © 1988, 2009 by Joyce Rupp. Used by permission of Ave Maria Press.

"Prayer for Those Experiencing Divorce" is reprinted from "Litany of Forgiveness" in *Prayers for Catholics Experiencing Divorce*, copyright © 2004 by Vicki Wells Bedard and William E. Rabior. Used by permission of Liguori Publications, www.ligouri.org.

"Prayer for Leaving Home" is reprinted from *Catholic Household Blessings and Prayers*, copyright © 1988 by The United States Catholic Conference Inc. Used by permission of USCCB Publishing.

✛

ESSAY
✢ CONTRIBUTORS ✢

Nicholas Ayo, C.S.C., is professor emeritus in the Program of Liberal Studies.

Sister Cynthia Broderick, O.P., is rector of Pasquerilla East.

Lawrence S. Cunningham is the John A. O'Brien professor of theology.

Brian Doyle is editor of *Portland Magazine* at the University of Portland.

John Dunne, C.S.C., is the John A. O'Brien professor of theology.

Virgilio Elizondo is professor of pastoral and Hispanic theology and a priest of the archdiocese of San Antonio.

David W. Fagerberg is associate professor of theology and director of the Notre Dame Center for Liturgy.

Michael Garvey is assistant director, Office of Public Affairs and Communication.

Sonia Gernes is professor emeritus of English.

Theodore M. Hesburgh, C.S.C., is president emeritus of the University of Notre Dame.

Lou Holtz was head football coach from 1986 to 1996.

John I. Jenkins, C.S.C., is president of the University of Notre Dame.

James B. King, C.S.C., is religious superior of Holy Cross Priests and Brothers at Notre Dame.

Renée LaReau is the web and multimedia specialist at the Kroc Institute for International Peace Studies.

Edward A. "Monk" Malloy, C.S.C., is president emeritus of the University of Notre Dame.

Timothy Matovina is professor of theology and the William and Anna Jean Cushwa Director of the Cushwa Center for the Study of American Catholicism.

Carol Ann Mooney is president of Saint Mary's College.

Colleen Moore is associate director of the Center for Catechetical Initiatives and Echo at the Institute for Church Life.

John Phalen, C.S.C., is president of Holy Cross Family Ministries in Massachusetts.

Gregory Ruehlmann is a contributing editor at Busted Halo.

Heidi Schlumpf teaches communication at Aurora University and is the editor of this volume.

Kristin Shrader-Frechette is the O'Neill Family endowed professor in the department of philosophy and department of biological sciences and the director of the Center for Environmental Justice and Children's Health.

Angela Sienko is the senior editor of alumni communications at Notre Dame.

Kerry Temple has been editor of *Notre Dame Magazine* since 1981.

Steven C. Warner is director of the Notre Dame Folk Choir.

Kenneth Woodward is a contributing editor of *Newsweek*, where he had been religion editor for thirty-eight years.

TITLES AND NAMES INDEX

✢ SUBJECT INDEX ✢

✛

Additional Ways to Pray in the Spirit of Notre Dame

Pray.nd.edu

An Initiative of the Notre Dame Alumni Association

Pray.nd.edu, created by the Notre Dame Alumni Association, is an online spiritual resource, offering a daily gospel reading and a brief reflection written by a member of the Notre Dame community. Visitors to Pray.nd.edu can submit a prayer request on the site. The Alumni Association staff responds to each prayer request and lights a candle at the Grotto.

www.ndprayercast.org®

NDPrayercast, a project of Notre Dame Campus Ministry, brings the spiritual vitality of the University of Notre Dame to the wider community through the Internet. Each week it provides several components: a greeting and introduction, a statement of focus for the week, a psalm reflection, the Sunday gospel reading and homily, a meditation song, intercessions, and the singing of the Lord's Prayer.